THE USES OF TALENT

THE USES
OF TALENT

By Dael Wolfle

LIBRARY

Princeton University Press
Princeton, New Jersey
1971

70160

Copyright © 1971 by Princeton University Press
ALL RIGHTS RESERVED
Library of Congress Card: 71-143817
International Standard Book Number: 0-691-08603-6

This book has been composed in Linotype Caledonia
Printed in the United States of America
by Princeton University Press, Princeton, New Jersey

LC
66
W6
copy 2

Contents

Foreword

THOSE FAMILIAR with his trenchant editorials in *Science*—and this group comprises the bulk of the scientific world both here and abroad—know of Dael Wolfle's concern over our unhappy profligacy with the nation's human resources and of his continuous effort to discover them and shepherd them into productive channels. Between 1950, the year marking the end of his highly productive tenure of the Executive Secretaryship of the American Psychological Association and his selection as Executive Officer of the American Association for the Advancement of Science (1954), he served as Director of the Commission on Human Resources and Advanced Training. It was during this four-year period that problems of identification and development of specialized talent became an absorbing interest with him. That it was also an abiding one has been amply shown in many ways. Beginning with the postwar realignment of science vis-à-vis the national need created by an exhausted scientific reserve, and continuing into the present period of excitement over long-range national goals, Dael Wolfle has literally been at the beck and call of all manner of agencies, public and private, concerned with manpower and its effective utilization.

It is only necessary to mention, among his many scholarly writings and editorial efforts, an earlier book, *America's Resources of Specialized Talent*, and his editorship of the volume, *The Discovery of Talent*, to suggest the appropriateness of *The Uses of Talent*. The lectures from which the book derived were delivered in late October and early November 1969, at Princeton University, and were made possible through the devotion and generosity of Mrs. Herbert S. Langfeld, of Princeton.

For the Herbert Sidney Langfeld
Memorial Lecture Committee,
FRANK A. GELDARD
Chairman

Acknowledgments

THE INVITATION to present the 1969 Herbert Sidney Langfeld lectures at Princeton University was a welcome one. It gave me the opportunity and the incentive to bring together the information and ideas set forth in the following chapters. I am grateful to Princeton University for the honor of being invited to help commemorate one of Princeton's distinguished professors.

My indebtedness to the staff of the Commission on Human Resources and Advanced Education is evident on many of the following pages. *Human Resources and Higher Education*, the Commission report written by John K. Folger, Helen Astin, and Alan Bayer, has now been published by the Russell Sage Foundation, which helped to support the work. Anyone seriously interested in the field should consult that report, for it contains much more information than I have included here on degree trends, career development, and related topics. Chapters Two and Four of this volume are largely based on *Human Resources and Higher Education*. My indebtedness goes beyond the citation of specific material; ideas were clarified and problems brought into focus by discussions with the authors, by reviewing the reports and drafts that preceded their final report, and by discussions with fellow members of the Commission, discussions that helped the staff plan and interpret their studies.

Another helpful group was the Committee on the International Migration of Talent. Their report has now been published by Education and World Affairs. Our concern with the studies conducted or sponsored by this committee was the range of problems that are inadequately, and somewhat incorrectly, categorized as the "brain drain." Although I have not given much attention to the international migration of talent here, our discussions of that topic helped to clarify some of my ideas concerning professional mobility.

Thanks are due for invitations from the University of Washington's Graduate School of Public Affairs and from the Battelle Memorial Institute in Seattle. I spent the winter of 1969 at the University of Washington, where I had the pleasure of leading a small seminar of faculty members and graduate students. The seminar discussions constituted a kind of first draft of what follows here. The final version benefited substantially from the questions and criticisms of my seminar colleagues.

Catherine Borras, who knows words, their usage, and English style far better than one has a right to expect in a secretary, has not only typed the successive drafts, but has also helped make each an improvement over its predecessor. Helen Wolfle, for long my most useful critic, has helped to remove errors of expression and thought. Both know how much I appreciate their willingness to be critical when there was still time to take advantage of criticism.

DAEL WOLFLE

Washington, D.C.
January 1970

THE USES OF TALENT

Introduction

W<small>HEN</small> Herodotus visited Egypt, 2400 years ago, he wrote of his surprise at the extent of medical specialization:

> Each physician treateth one part and not more. And everywhere is full of physicians; for some profess themselves physicians of the eyes, and others of the head, and others of the teeth, and others of the parts about the belly, and others of obscure sicknesses.[1]

These few lines tell much about the advanced state of Egyptian civilization. Twenty-four hundred years ago they could not possibly have been written of what is now London, or Paris, or Princeton. Only in reference to advanced civilizations with considerable division of labor would such a statement be credible. Today we would accept a similar account of medical practice in London or New York, but not of that in a primitive area or pioneer community.

From these few lines we can also make some assumptions about Egyptian medical specialists. They must have been brighter than the average Egyptian and better educated. These are characteristics typical of physicians and people who occupy other specialized and professional positions in society.

Specialists and professionals are the kind of people about whom this book is written. They are not the part of the total population that is now of most immediate

[1] *The History of Herodotus*, trans. J. Enoch Powell, Oxford, Clarendon Press, 1949; book II, chapter 84.

social concern. For very sound reasons, American society is giving much more attention than it ever has in the past to the impoverished, the disadvantaged, the victims of racial discrimination, the members of minority groups, and others who have not shared fully in the affluence and advantages of the American system.

I am not going to follow this theme. I do not disagree with it: I applaud it. We would all be far better off if a hundred years ago we had been aroused to the concern we now feel, but this is not my topic. I shall not, however, forget these groups, for within them are young people whose high potential talent never fully develops, and I will have to pay attention to that point.

My emphasis will be on the people who are bright regardless of family background, the people who get educated whatever the level of their parents' education, the people who work at responsible positions in the professions and specialized fields. For all of us, including those who lack the advantages of education and high ability, this is an important segment of the total population, and it is this part of the population to which I have devoted a good deal of time in the past twenty years. It is, therefore, this group, and the young people who may become qualified to join it, that is my subject.

In the chapters that follow, I shall be looking at three different aspects of this group of people. First, there are the people themselves. How many are there? Who are they? Who benefits and who is left out? Have they changed significantly over recent decades? Are we satisfied with the customs and policies which determine who gains access to the educational and occupational advantages of specialization and the professions, or do we wish to make some changes?

Second, there is the question of ends and purposes. We have a set of institutions that educate people of high ability, and we have another set of institutions in which we use their talents to produce goods and services for society. Are we using these two sets of institutions to achieve the purposes that have highest priority in American life? If we change the goals or objectives, how will we affect the people involved and the means we use to educate and employ their talents?

Finally, there are the means themselves: the institutions and the customs and policies that determine how the United States accomplishes the business of educating and utilizing able people.

Although I have listed the means third, after the people involved and after the objectives served, I shall treat this aspect first. Chapter One will briefly describe the system we operate in America and call attention to some of the major problems that will require some changes in the ways in which it operates. Here I should make explicit my prejudice concerning the system of institutions and customs through which we educate and utilize men and women of ability. I have confidence in the essential soundness of this system and in its ability to evolve constructively. Not everyone agrees. Some critics see the faults clearly but have difficulty seeing the virtues. Other critics, probably fewer in number but more vigorous in tone, want to tear the whole system down in the hope that a fresh start would lead to something better. Faults there surely are, and some are glaring. Yet the faults are not so fundamental as to require abandoning the whole system. It has proven its flexibility by correcting earlier faults and by adapting to past changes. It can do so now.

Chapter Two will summarize some of the major trends of supply and demand, for we are now at a time when some of the supply-demand relationships are changing rapidly.

Chapter Three will review some of the analyses that have been made of the benefits of college education, benefits both for the individuals and for society.

Chapter Four will concentrate on the people involved and on the factors that determine who does and who does not gain the benefits of higher education and thus get into the specialized and professional fields.

Chapter Five will focus on the same people, after they leave the college or university. The United States differs significantly from most other countries in the kinds of linkages which exist between a person's education and his field of work, and in the great extent to which occupational mobility is used to adjust the available supply of educated specialists to the various kinds of work society wants done.

Finally, in Chapter Six, I want to describe a major shortcoming of the present arrangements and discuss some of the options we will have in our uses of talent.

Much thought has been given to the analysis of how we produce, distribute, and use our physical resources—raw materials, money, and manufactured products. The comparable analysis of how we produce, distribute, and utilize human resources is not nearly as well advanced, despite a great deal of writing on individual parts of this realm. The literature on education is vast. There is no lack of material on management. There is a rapidly increasing and substantial number of books and articles on the economics of education. One of the most precise and perhaps the most widely useful of the branches of psychology has been the analysis and measurement of human abilities. Sociologists have contributed substantially to an understanding of the conditions that foster or impede human development.

Some of the information and some of the ideas from these various sources can be brought together—I hope usefully—in a discussion of the system we have developed to identify, develop, deploy, and utilize engineers, lawyers, scientists, and the educated and talented members of other professions and specialties. It would be presumptuous indeed to call the result a science of human resources. It is far from being ready for that label. But my purpose is to make a start in the direction of bringing the parts together into a meaningful whole.

In considering the forces that determine how we educate and utilize men and women of high ability, it is necessary to distinguish between the point of view of the individual and the point of view of society. In 1776, when Adam Smith published *An Inquiry into the Nature and Causes of the Wealth of Nations*, he emphasized the role of education, competence, and skill as the bases of national wealth. He was ahead of his time in taking this position. Later economists were more impressed with physical capital than they were with human capital.

Now, however, knowledge has become the principal economic resource in the advanced countries, and it promises to become even more important, relative to other resources, in the newly emerging industries and services.[2] Consequently, the economic importance of education has become widely recognized, the concept of human capital has gained currency, and the economics of education has become one of the fastest growing branches of economics.[3]

As a result of these changes in economic thought, the literature of education, economics, and national development has come to be peppered with such terms as "human capital," "human resources," "investment in man," and others that seem to treat man as a commodity to be shaped and manipulated, much as one manufactures a product or uses physical capital.

I must explain and apologize to those who shudder at the thought of treating human beings in all their rich variety as if they were capital to be manipulated for social purposes. We do not think of ourselves so. No one ever answered the question "Who are you?" by saying, "I am one unit of the nation's human capital." Of course not. From his standpoint, our systems of education and employment are for the individual to use for his own betterment. And this, in large measure, is why we have developed our educational system as we have. Yet that educational system and our labor market mechanisms are also the means by which we educate and utilize talent for the purposes society has set for itself. It is therefore as legitimate to examine the processes in-

[2] Peter F. Drucker, *The Age of Discontinuity*, New York, Harper and Row, 1968. Drucker presents a valuable and provocative discussion of this proposition.

[3] Mark Blaug, *Economics of Education*, vol. 1, Baltimore, Maryland, Penguin Books (Penguin Education X56), 1968. Blaug opens his introduction with the statement: "Ten years ago there was hardly such a subject as the economics of education. Today it is one of the most rapidly growing branches of economics." The volume consists of selected papers from the growing literature of this field.

8

volved from the standpoint of society as it is to consider them from the standpoint of the individual.

The individual view is the right one for an individual, or his friends or family, to take. He is interested in what will be best for him. Should he go to college? Which college? Will he be happier or more productive in this job or in that one? These are the kinds of questions to ask when a student is considering how he can best use the educational opportunities that are open to him for his own development and to his own advantage. These are primary questions, and in the last analysis the educational system will be judged on the basis of how well it meets the needs of students.

There is, however, another set of equally legitimate questions. University presidents, the United States Commissioner of Education, members of Congress, and state legislators are responsible for the allocation of budgets that are never large enough to satisfy all demands. From the societal point of view which they must adopt, it is proper to ask whether the universities are educating enough doctors or engineers or school teachers. And it is necessary to engage in an increasing amount of forward planning of educational facilities and opportunities, both to satisfy the expected student demand and also to satisfy the expected needs of the nation.

The two views are not opposed. They are complementary. Moreover, their objectives are congruent. Students have several reasons for going to college, but a common and powerful one is vocational preparation. In graduate and professional school this is the dominant reason. Society has several reasons for supporting higher education, but educating the necessary specialists is a major one.

Whether the individual or the societal point of view is the more appropriate depends upon the questions being asked. I shall use whichever one better fits the topic being considered.

1. The Ecology of Specialization

SPECIALIZATION develops in cities. Adam Smith pointed out long ago that the clumping together of people permitted substantial division of labor and gave rise to occupational and professional specialization. Complex patterns of culture are found in agrarian societies, but the number of different occupational roles is limited. Specialization is a characteristic of complex societies. It grows as cities grow, and it continues to increase as a society moves along the road of technological advancement and economic development.

In the United States, differentiation continues. The Bureau of the Census periodically increases the number of categories used in classifying professional and technical occupations. Several years ago the Bureau announced that the occupational classifications used in 1960 will no longer suffice and that finer breakdowns will be used in the 1970 census.

From Herodotus to Adam Smith to the Bureau of the Census there is evidence for what can be called the first principle of occupational specialization: as a society advances economically and culturally, the number of occupational specialties increases. As the number of specialists grows, the total range of work to be performed also increases, and this is indeed a reason for specialization. But as the number of specialties increases, each one claims a smaller segment of the total range of work to be performed. In medicine, general practitioners have largely given way to pediatricians, psychiatrists, thoracic surgeons, and other specialists. A church that used to have one minister now has several,

11

including a minister for youth and a minister for music. Instead of physicists we have atomic physicists, solid-state physicists, nuclear physicists, and still others. And in psychology there are clinical, counseling, social, experimental, comparative, and other kinds of psychologists.

The various occupational specialties depend upon each other and influence each other. Lawyers and ministers and engineers, bankers and salesmen and school teachers, and people in all the rest of the professional and specialized occupations interact in an intricate web of overlapping relationships. They aid and support and supplement each other. Sometimes they compete. Some specialized groups exist solely to serve other specialized groups. There is a constant flow of information among them, and various external controls and feedback mechanisms tend, although often imperfectly, to keep their numbers in reasonable balance with each other and with the needs of society.

A thumbnail sketch of the state of specialization in the United States today would include the following points. The number of professional and specialized fields is large and is still growing. As the number of identifiable specialties increases, the portion of the whole spectrum of socially useful work claimed by each specialty grows narrower. As knowledge increases, so do specialization and the time required to become a fully accredited specialist. As knowledge increases and is applied to the production of goods and services, wealth increases, as does the demand for persons of high ability and advanced education. This is where the United States is now, as far along the road of increasing specialization as any nation in the world, and farther than most.

Although this is where we are now, the description is incomplete. It would have been sufficient until a few years ago, but now it is necessary to warn that major changes are occurring in several of the forces and institutions that determine how we educate and employ the ablest members of society.

Major Factors in the Development and Utilization of Talent

If "system" had not come to be identified with what many thoughtful persons find objectionable in the way the affairs of the United States are managed, and if we were more systematic in the means we use to identify talented persons and to develop and utilize their abilities, it would be appropriate to speak of the "Talent Development and Utilization System of the United States." But if there is such a system, it is not very systematic, and if it were, the objections to it would be even stronger than they are now.

The fact is that we have no centrally planned and systematically controlled system. What we have is a number of institutions and processes that together result in preparing people for specialized fields of work and in making use of their knowledge and abilities. All of these institutions and processes are familiar, but it is not usual to treat them together, because their analysis has traditionally been divided among several different disciplines. They can be grouped under four headings.

Educational Institutions. Here are included all schools, from kindergarten through professional and graduate schools and even postdoctoral and mid-career educational programs. Not only the institutions themselves, but also the educational processes and their out-

13

comes, have been studied chiefly by psychologists and educators. In the last decade, there has also been a vigorous invasion of this area by economists interested in the economics of education.

The Employment Sector. All of the jobs we generate to employ the talents and reward the accomplishments of men and women of ability are included here. These jobs have been of principal interest to labor-market economists, management specialists, and sociologists.

Individual Choices. This sector includes the factors that determine how individuals use the educational and occupational opportunities open to them. The decisions of individuals about their own education and careers, and the factors that help to determine those decisions, have been studied primarily by sociologists, demographers, and psychologists.

Formulation of Policy. Here are the decision-making processes that influence or control educational and occupational opportunities and that are intended to influence educational and occupational choices. The study of these governmental and policy factors falls chiefly within the realm of the political scientists.

Political scientists, educators, psychologists, sociologists, management specialists, demographers, and economists all have an interest in these institutions and processes, but no discipline claims responsibility for all the problems involved, and there has been no real effort to integrate all of the parts into a conceptual whole. The principal parts are all known, however, and it is possible to fit them together into a scheme or model that shows the major components and relationships.

Figure 1 presents, in bare outline, the principal ele-

14

ments of this model. The left-hand portion represents the whole range of formal educational institutions, from kindergarten on up. Education used to be almost exclusively the province of schools and colleges. With advances in knowledge, increasing specialization, and the faster obsolescence of what one learns in college, more and more of the responsibility for education is shifting to the postcollege years. The postdoctoral fellow has become a familiar figure on the university campus. Refresher courses and opportunities to spend time in advanced study during mid-career years are increasingly recognized to be essential to the full develop-

Figure 1
A Model of the Education and Utilization of Talent
in the United States

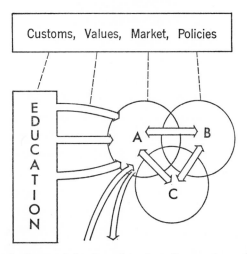

Generalized schema of the flow of students from various educational levels to occupation A; the flow of workers into and out of occupation A and among occupations A, B, and C; and the customs, values, market conditions, and policies that influence these movements of students and workers.

ment and maintenance of human talent. In fact, the education and utilization of high talent has become a life-long process and is decreasingly one that can be divided into two distinct phases. One evidence is the large amount of money industry now spends on training programs for its professional and executive personnel. The size of this sum is quite uncertain, for there is no central collection of information on the matter, but estimates run from, say, $4 or $5 billion a year upwards.

The Training of Talent

Although education and utilization overlap and sometimes alternate in time, it is appropriate to separate the period of formal education from the period of utilization, because the two are guided and controlled by different policy-making machinery and because students and professional workers think of themselves as being in different stages of their careers.

After varying amounts of education, streams of students leave the educational stage and flow into professional and specialized fields of work. For some professions, college graduation is the typical time for making this change, while in other fields a graduate or professional degree is the customary prerequisite. In no profession, however, is there a single, fixed level of education which is attained by all new entrants. The minimum entering level may be rigidly established, as it is in medicine, but the maximum entering level is not. In all professional and specialized fields there is a range of educational preparation that qualifies a new entrant for admission.

In the future, students of varying quality, and after

varying numbers of years of study, will leave the university to begin their postcollege careers. But in some ways the universities and colleges will operate and function somewhat differently in the years ahead than they have in recent decades. This is abundantly clear from the pressures on higher education and from the number of current efforts to improve it, or perhaps only to change it.

One problem is money. Universities and colleges are in deep financial trouble. So, for that matter, is the whole educational system, from kindergarten to graduate school. The voters of many communities have refused to authorize bond issues for new school construction or have refused to raise tax limits to allow states and cities to increase their educational budgets. State legislatures have reduced by many millions of dollars the requests submitted on behalf of state universities and colleges. Federal appropriations for education and especially for science seem to have a harder and harder time getting through Congress and the President's office.

There is reason for this balkiness on the part of citizens and legislators. The costs of education have been growing more rapidly than the population, more rapidly than the Gross National Product, more rapidly than inflation, and too rapidly to continue. In the decade of the 1960's, the population of the United States increased by 14 percent. During that same decade, elementary school enrollment also increased by 14 percent, but high school enrollment went up 55 percent, and college and university enrollment doubled. The costs of education climbed even more rapidly. In a decade in

17

which college and university enrollment grew by 104 percent, expenditures for higher education rose by 186 percent, and state legislatures increased by 250 percent the tax funds appropriated for higher education. All told, our colleges and universities now cost more than twenty billion dollars a year, and this amount represents twice as large a fraction of the Gross National Product as was spent on higher education from the much smaller GNP of ten years ago.

In the United States, as well as in a number of other countries, the percentage of the Gross National Product that is devoted to higher education has reached a level that looks to many legislators and government officials to be about as high as can be justified. We are a wealthy nation, and we can expect educational budgets to continue to increase. Nevertheless, we must expect a financial pinch, particularly in higher education. That is where the cost per student is greatest and where campus turmoil is most likely to lead to punitive responses from the state capitals or from Washington. The Carnegie Commission on Higher Education thinks that the higher-education budget should go up to $41 billion by 1976-77. A great many legislators and taxpayers are likely to consider that too much. Universities will surely be squeezed between pressures to admit more students and offer them expensive new programs and services and pressures to keep costs from getting out of bounds.

Universities are also in trouble over the charge that some of their effort is misdirected. There is, for example, a growing conviction on the part of many people that too often the goals of the specialist conflict with the goals of society, and that where such conflict exists, the goals of society must prevail. Those who hold this view are fed up with the policy of "business as usual," in a university as much as in an automobile factory. They assert that educational programs, as well as governmental and industrial programs, must be more deliberately and consciously planned in terms of the long-range welfare of society as a whole.

One manifestation of this attitude is the rebellion against the military-industrial complex, or the research-oriented university, or the alleged domination of man by his technological achievements. Another exemplification is the expressed wish for better integration of the work of different specialties. Thus, stronger interdisciplinary linkages are called for, as are social engineers, family physicians, and other generalists who can direct and integrate the work of a variety of more specialized specialists.

In their more extreme forms, the accusations against the university would destroy some of its basic purposes. Colleges and universities must satisfy the diverse wishes of students, some of whom come to college for strictly vocational purposes, some of whom come with other educational aspirations, and some of whom come with still different ideas of how they want to spend their college years. At the same time, colleges and universities are expected to educate approximately the right numbers of specialists to serve the needs of society. If one took seriously the claim that universities should cease preparing men and women for professional and specialized roles in society, it would immediately become necessary to create new institutions to educate the doctors, lawyers, scientists, diplomats, engineers,

19

THE USES OF TALENT

scholars, and other specialists and leaders that society needs.

How much American colleges and universities today emphasize the education of young people as they want to be educated and how much they emphasize the training of people to take places in the established order of commerce, industry, government, and higher education is a subject of much contemporary argument. Universities are sometimes accused of not having the interests of the students at heart, but of serving instead as a tool of the established order, functioning to produce new cogs for the machinery of society. In his valedictory address at Princeton in June 1969, Michael Bernstein expressed this charge in saying, "What we resent is feeling that we are being educated only to fulfill some predetermined role in society."[1]

Granted that the universities must serve both the wishes of students and the needs of society—that they must prepare students for the kinds of jobs that are expected to exist and must educate them for whatever their personal objectives may be—it is important to remember that the size of the whole higher educational effort is determined primarily by student demand and not by national planning, and that the relative emphasis on different subjects and courses is also determined primarily by student demand. In this respect the United States differs significantly from many other countries. Elsewhere it is not uncommon for official planning bodies to forecast the need for engineers (to take that profession as an example) and then to provide the number of places in engineering schools that will produce

[1] Michael A. Bernstein, *University: A Princeton Quarterly*, Fall 1969.

the required number of graduates. In the United States, we operate our higher educational institutions primarily on the basis of meeting student demands rather than meeting the requirements of national plans and forecasts.

This characteristic of American educational policy not only affects students and universities but also determines the nature of the linkage between education and work and influences the ways in which graduates are later employed and the ease and frequency with which they change employment.

Jobs To Utilize Trained Talent

The second major part of the model consists of all the jobs that are generated to utilize educated men and women. The professional and specialized working force is divided into a large number of more or less distinct but clearly overlapping categories and subcategories. All exhibit continuing inward and outward flows of several kinds. Beginners flow into each field after varying amounts of educational preparation. Older workers leave because of retirement, death, or illness. Some who leave return later. Moreover, workers switch from one field of specialization to another as their interests change or as they see better opportunities in new fields of work.

This last kind of transfer, from one specialty to another, violates the stereotype of a student who decides upon the field of work he thinks most attractive, prepares for entry by taking the appropriate courses or curricula, enters his chosen field, and remains there for the rest of his career. Some people do follow such straight-line courses through life. But there are twists

21

and turns in the career lines of many others, and this is particularly true in the United States. American students are more likely than their foreign counterparts to change their majors while in college. The linkage between college curricula and postcollege work is looser in the United States than in, say, France, England, or Japan.

Whether college and university graduates follow straight courses or twisted ones, if they are to realize their professional aspirations and if society is to benefit from its investment in their education, appropriate jobs must be available when they receive their degrees and start to look for work.

If there is not a reasonable match between educational preparation and work opportunities, trouble is sure to follow. If the universities graduate too few qualified students, there are manpower shortages, and some socially important work either does not get done or gets done at undue cost or sacrifice elsewhere in society.

If the universities graduate too many, there is also trouble. This is the situation which worries some of the poorer countries of the world, countries that have bet so heavily on the economic values of higher education as to become educationally overextended. The aspirations of their students have been encouraged by hopes of a bright future and rapid economic development, and these aspirations have been fostered by assistance, in building schools and colleges, from advanced countries and international agencies. Too often, the result has been that the educational system has rushed ahead of the ability of the economy to absorb the graduates.

Starting from a comparatively low base, as the developing countries have done, it is not difficult to increase the number of university graduates by, say, 10 percent a year. But it is difficult to expand the economy by more than about 4 percent a year. A flow increasing at a 10 percent rate poured into a vessel that is growing at a 4 percent rate is bound to result in a spillover. And that is exactly what is happening. University graduates who cannot be absorbed in Taiwan, or the Philippines, or India, or Pakistan are migrating to the United States, to England, and to other countries in which jobs are more plentiful and attractive than they are at home.

Emigration is a possibility here, too. Generally, the flow of Americans to Canada is smaller than the flow of Canadians to the United States, but in some fields it is approximately equivalent. There are almost as many American economists teaching in Canada as there are Canadian economists teaching in the United States.[2] More than 20 percent of the psychologists with doctoral degrees in Canada are United States citizens.[3]

Emigration sometimes provides an escape route for university graduates who cannot find suitable jobs at home. But the emigration route is not open to all. Nor is it the only consequence of educating more men and women than can find suitable jobs. In some countries, substantial numbers of university graduates are unemployed, and even larger numbers are employed in jobs well below their capacities. These are conditions that are almost sure to lead to social unrest.

[2] Herbert B. Grubel and A. D. Scott, "The International Flow of Human Capital," *American Economic Review*, vol. 56, no. 2 (1966): 268-74.

[3] W. R. Dymond and K. V. Pankhurst, "Studies of Highly Qualified Manpower in the Canadian Department of Manpower and Immigration," Paper presented at the Cornell University Conference on Human Mobility, Ithaca, New York, Oct. 31–Nov. 2, 1968.

In short, the generalization is justified that any country can expect trouble if it does not maintain a reasonable balance between the numbers of persons educated for the specialized professions and the ability of the economy to provide them with suitable employment.

The United States has largely avoided this kind of trouble, and for this fortunate circumstance much of the credit must go to an educational policy that has fostered general education, and to an occupational policy that has fostered a higher level of mobility than is to be found elsewhere.

Millions of Decisions

The educational sector is coupled with the occupational sector by millions upon millions of decisions made by millions of people. All but a few of these decisions are made independently; often they are based on incomplete or inaccurate information; and most are made for personal rather than for social or national reasons. Yet collectively this multiplicity of decisions determines whether there will be a good or a poor match between the numbers of persons educated in the various specialized fields and the ability of the economy to provide them with suitable positions.

The decisions of teachers, faculties, and administrators, about courses, curricula, and educational policies are all involved. Also involved are the decisions of students to study or not to study, to take this course or that one, to stay in school or to drop out. Later on these same people will be deciding to leave one job and take another, to take advantage of an opportunity for special training, or to retire. Their employers also make de-

24

cisions: to expand or contract, to support a research program, or to market a new product. And there are decisions made by government agencies to increase or decrease educational appropriations, to provide more money for urban renewal, to increase taxes, or to abolish military deferments for graduate students.

Collectively, with good effects or disturbing ones, the Board of Regents' decision to establish a new branch of the University of California, an industrialist's decision to locate a plant in Trenton, John Doe's decision to accept that job in Denver, his daughter's decision to major in history, the decision of Congress to reduce the number of graduate fellowships, and millions upon millions of other decisions determine how we educate and how we use talent in the United States.

If this description makes the whole process seem disorderly and lacking in neatness and logical planning, that is the way it is. Observers from other countries sometimes criticize our system as costly, wasteful, and irrational; it is nonetheless our system. We will try to improve it, but we are not likely to abandon it. If the description makes it sound as if talent development and utilization depend upon everything else that goes on, that too is the way it is. Human talent is used everywhere in society, and every facet of society has an influence on how it is developed and used.

Simplification and abstraction are of course necessary in order to analyze the processes involved, and the great multitude of decisions can be divided into two broad categories: the decisions of individuals concerning their own lives and the policy decisions that help determine the nature of the educational and occupational opportunities available. Both kinds of decisions are influenced by customs and values; both are part of the mechanisms of the labor market; and there is much interaction between them. Yet the two kinds of decisions are made by different people, for different reasons, and should therefore be discussed separately. They constitute the third and fourth sectors, which are shown, quite figuratively, at the top of Figure 1.

Individuals and Their Career Decisions

American concern for freedom of choice is evident throughout the whole realm of talent development and utilization. After a minimum age, students are free to continue in school or to drop out. For those who continue, there are enough schools of enough different kinds to permit each to go as far as he likes in the directions of his own choice. After he decides he has had enough schooling, he is free to take or to reject any job offered him and to change jobs as frequently as he likes. Other choices come later. Men change jobs. Women leave the labor force and then return. Workers move geographically. They change from one kind of work to another. Sometimes they even change from one field of specialization to another.

All of this is part of the American system of values, but we have fallen far short of its universal realization. As a result of a lot of human frailty and some entrenched discrimination, the opportunity to enjoy complete freedom of educational choice has been closely correlated with the color of a person's skin. There have been other lapses from the ideal. In times of danger, individual rights have sometimes been suspended—as when conditions of war required conscription. And yet the ideal remains. Despite past and present failures, the high value we place on individual freedom of opportunity and our insistence on the individual's right to develop to the fullness of his own wishes and potentials powerfully influence the specific practices we have developed for educating and utilizing talent.

Policy Decisions

We like to think that both supply and demand have been left to the operation of a freely operating market. On the supply side, freedom of individual choice is still our avowed policy, and with the shortcomings and limitations already mentioned, our practice approximates what we preach. Although students and workers are free to do as they wish, the federal government increasingly tries to influence students to choose fields in which the nation needs more men. When government-supported fellowships were made available to graduate students in the sciences, but not in other disciplines, the purpose was obvious, and the justification that persuaded Congress to appropriate the money was the expectation that the nation would need more scientists than would be available without the graduate fellowships. In the past dozen years, comparable programs, with comparable supporting arguments, have provided financial support for prospective college teachers, guidance workers, and medical personnel.

Under our free enterprise system, the demand side of the market also used to be comparatively free, but the demand for specialized talent has been increasingly coming under centralized control. Industrial trends are

27

a powerful force toward centrality. As giant corporations have replaced many small entrepreneurs, and as more and more government controls have been adopted, we have moved farther and farther from a completely free economy. John Kenneth Galbraith has developed this thesis in his book *The New Industrial State*.[4]

Governmental trends also push toward centrality. Central government decisions have created or expanded, and have sometimes curtailed, large segments of the job market. Defense expenditures are the largest and the national space effort is probably the most spectacular example of government influence, but there are other, less spectacular, forms. Changing federal appropriations for research and development create or change demands for scientists and engineers. The collection and dissemination of economic statistics and the projection of economic and manpower trends shape commercial and industrial decisions.

A special example of the governmental role is the decision that some kind of service is a right of all Americans. When we declare something to be a human right, we largely take it off the market. The classic example is education itself. The adoption of Medicare and Medicaid legislation provides a more recent example.

If by policy we mean the practices we actually follow, rather than the traditional statements we repeat on ceremonial occasions, our national policy with respect to supply and demand in the specialized and professional fields reduces to an interesting disjuncture. On the sup-

[4] John Kenneth Galbraith, *The New Industrial State,* Boston, Houghton Mifflin Co., 1967.

ply side we still try to run a free market. There are barriers of color and poverty that close off educational opportunities to some people, and there are national programs that are intended to increase the supply in selected fields. Nevertheless, each student and worker has a great deal of freedom to do as he pleases. The supply of professional and specialized manpower is, therefore, largely determined by individual choice. But the jobs that are available, or the demand for specialized services, are increasingly determined centrally and nationally.

Whether this somewhat disjointed system is judged to have worked well or to have worked poorly can be argued. From the individual viewpoint, it has worked well for a majority, and poorly for a minority. From the collective viewpoint of society, its benefits have outweighed its faults, but some of the faults are glaring. However one rates it now, the system is heading into trouble.

Transition and Change

Every time is a time of transition from what has gone before to what will follow, but in some periods the changes are particularly large, or swift, or disturbing. We are now at such a stage with respect to the uses of talent. It is in fact the simultaneity of several major changes of direction or emphasis that makes this a particularly appropriate time for a critical analysis of the means we use to educate and utilize men and women of talent.

I have already pointed out two important changes. First, the growth rate of funds for higher education has slowed down. We are surely past the time of most rapid increase in federal appropriations for scientific research and development and almost surely past the time of most rapid increase of total appropriations for higher education. Second, the universities are suffering through an agonizing period of self-analysis of their responsibilities and their relations with governmental and social problems.

Three more changes are relevant. One is that we are past the stage of most rapid expansion of need in a number of fields. We are moving from a sellers' market to a buyers' market in several fields of specialization. We are also in the process of moving from the industrial society of past decades to what Daniel Bell calls the "post-industrial society," or what Peter Drucker calls the "knowledge society." We do not yet know all of the characteristics of this change or its implications for individual careers. But clearly it is taking a smaller and smaller fraction of the working force to produce all the food and clothing and goods and gadgets we need, with the result that more and more college graduates will be able to do other things. It is also clear that more and more of what they will be doing depends upon systematic knowledge and its application rather than upon experience in the traditional ways of working. This transition poses some perplexing problems for educational planning.

Finally, we are moving into an age in which we will deliberately plan for the future. We do not have much experience; we do not yet have adequate institutional organizations for future planning; and some of the plans will no doubt turn out badly. Nevertheless, we can take it for granted that much more than in the past we will set national goals and will plan their funding levels and manpower requirements. The market will not be put out of business, but we can expect that in the future a larger number of the jobs to be performed by educated men and women will be parts of large-scale, nationally planned efforts to achieve national goals.

Taken together, these five changes will result in changes in higher education, in the demand for college graduates, in the need for education, and in the responsibilities of different professions.

An Ecological Analogy

I have called this chapter "The Ecology of Specialization" to emphasize the dynamic and changing relationships among the fields of specialization and to call attention to the dependence of the extent and nature of specialization upon the environment in which it develops. A number of the characteristics of specialization and of the relations among fields of specialization can be described in the same terms as the development of a biological ecosystem, a plant and animal community. If we speak of species instead of specialties, if we call their roles niches instead of specializations, and if we say that the number of species increases as the ecosystem matures, then we have described some well-recognized ecological trends.[5]

---

[5] Eugene P. Odum, "The Strategy of Ecosystem Development," *Science*, 164 (1969): 262-70. Dr. Odum discusses the transitions from early to mature ecosystems and even labels one section of his article "Relevance of Ecosystem Developmental Theory to Human Ecology." His excellent article stimulated my analogy, but he has no responsibility for the way in which I have used it.

On land that has been plowed and then allowed to lie fallow, or on a mountain side that has been swept by a forest fire, one can watch the development of a new ecological system. The first plants to appear are hardy, fast-growing weeds. Ragweed, fireweed, jack pine, or other plants of low repute come first. At this pioneer stage, the plants grow rapidly, and quantity of production is more evident than quality. There are only a few different species, and in order to survive, the early arrivals must be adaptable to a considerable range of soil and temperature and moisture conditions. Like human beings who move into a new world, they are pioneers, and like any other Jack-of-all-trades, they have to fill broad portions of the whole web of interrelationships in the new community. Later on, more species are found. Each fills a more specialized niche. The emphasis is on quality rather than quantity of growth, and along with this change there is a marked deceleration of the growth rate. In a mature forest one finds slow-growing oaks and hickories and chestnuts or, in a different climate, redwoods and Douglas firs.

The men and women who came to Jamestown and Plymouth were also pioneers. They were Jacks-of-all-trades instead of highly differentiated specialists. The men who rushed to California and later to Alaska, drawn by the lure of gold, were of a similar breed. They dug prospect holes, cut timber, built sluice boxes, shoveled muck, panned gold, hunted and cooked their own food, and did whatever else needed doing. Their occupational specialty was pioneering. As development continues, men come to fill more specialized niches, the number of specialties increases, preparation for specialized work takes long years of education, and oak-like quality instead of pine-like speed of growth is emphasized.

The emphasis on quality tends to squeeze out those who cannot compete. In a forest ecosystem, some species that grew well in the earlier stages can no longer survive in the later stages. We are not always so ruthless in a human society, but we have the same kind of problem. It is the ignorant, the uneducated, and those of marginal ability who can find no jobs in a technologically advanced society. And the margin of unsuitability moves up as life gets more complex. An I.Q. of 70 used to mark the borderline separating the mentally retarded from the normal. A few years ago the National Association for Mental Retardation moved the borderline up to an I.Q. of 85. Persons with I.Q.'s between 70 and 85 could get along reasonably well in the simpler world of yesterday, but not in today's world.

There is another major difference between the young stages of an ecological succession and the mature stage. The mature stage is more stable, more resistant to disturbing influences. A cornfield or an apple orchard can be wrecked by a single species of pest. A climax forest is much more resistant. The stability of a mature ecosystem is somehow a consequence of the diversity of species that make up the system. Societies show a similar contrast between concentration and instability on the one hand and diversity and stability on the other. The dust bowl farmers of our own history, the one-company town, the banana republics and the coffee-growing regions of Latin America are highly vulnerable to changes in weather or in the market. The much more varied agricultural-industrial-service-financial-techno-

33

logical society of a modern state or region has its ups and downs, but the swings are less catastrophic than the boom-and-bust cycles of more homogeneous societies and areas.

Man the destroyer has been responsible for the principal exceptions to this generalization. In ancient times he deforested Mediterranean hills and in modern times his wastes have ruined Lake Erie. Wherever man has been most abundant and most "progressive" there he has also been most destructive of mature forest, prairie, lake, and estuarine ecosystems, on a scale more massive and lasting than that produced by floods, fire, or most other natural catastrophes. Nevertheless, except for human destruction, the generalization holds: a mature and balanced ecosystem is more adaptable to change than is a young ecosystem.

In an ecological community, the cause-and-effect relationships are not well understood, but the fact seems clear that maintenance and homeostasis require a large number of species. Probably the great range of genetic variability, stored within each species, that is available whenever environmental changes put a premium on evolutionary adaptation is also involved. In human societies, diversity of specialization and variability within each specialized and professional group seem to be adaptive. But whether this similarity between the two kinds of communities represents only a semantic parallelism or indicates a more fundamental unity of biological and social organizations, I do not know.

In a biological ecosystem, the climax stage is marked by great stability: change is slow; ecological flux is at a minimum. Here the analogy breaks down. American society has not reached its climax stage; it is still evolving. Yet we know enough now to realize that we have some control over our own social evolution. In a number of dimensions we are far enough along to know that we should begin to plan for the kind of mature society we want to attain.

Thus, in a curious way, perhaps the analogy to a climax state will be closer in a few decades than it is now. We do have an opportunity to decide on the kind of climax state we want to reach, and already there is much thinking going on that can help in making the decision. This new kind of thinking has several bases. Most obvious is the realization that we cannot allow population growth to continue unchecked. Sooner or later, and the sooner the better, we must reach a state of zero population growth—a stable, climax population that may vary up or down a bit but must not go on climbing.

Another reason for giving greater thought to the future is the growing realization that we can no longer allow technology to continue unchecked. We have become frightened by the extent to which we have polluted our environment, insulted our senses, and damaged our health. Society is moving now, slowly as yet but in a variety of ways, to check and monitor and plan technological developments to maximize their benefits and minimize or counteract their harmful side effects. Stated in positive terms, what we are beginning to seek is the arrangements that will allow a stable population to live in permanently balanced harmony with the natural environment the Earth provides.

There is a third reason for increased efforts to see into the future and to guide future trends. Through most of man's long history, the changes that lay ahead, even if unforeseen, were much vaster than the changes of the past. This history shapes our attitudes toward the future. Sunday journalists like to predict that the changes of the next twenty years will be far greater than the changes of the past twenty. In some ways perhaps they will be. In some of our domestic and international arrangements, we hope for much more rapid improvement in the future than in the past. But in a number of significant ways the rate of change is bound to slow down. The time to travel from Princeton to Santa Barbara will be about the same in 1990 as it is now. The speed of communication over great distances will get no faster than it was on July 20, 1969, when Neil Armstrong took his first step on the Moon. The percentage of the population engaged in agriculture has almost reached its minimum. Cities will change in character and we may individually choose to live in large cities or smaller ones, but we have become a nation of townsmen, and we will continue to want the specialized services that cities provide.

In some other respects, the rate of change will also slow down. Going to high school used to be the exception rather than the rule. Now nearly every boy and girl starts high school and 80 percent graduate. We have thought of college as being for the minority. But over half of all young men and over 40 percent of all young women of freshman age now enroll in college. The percentage is still increasing annually, but one does not have to look very far into the future to see the time approaching when college enrollment will no longer be increasing rapidly.

36

In the near future, things will still be in a state of considerable flux, but much attention will be devoted to national goals and to planning the kind of society we want. How we make these decisions, which goals we choose to emphasize, has a clear and obvious bearing on the numbers of people needed in the various specialties and the kinds of work they will be called upon to do.

In the more distant future, we can expect something approaching a climax-state society. Never before has it made sense to speak in such terms. From the beginning of man until very recently, human evolution has been essentially passive, and although man has done much to change his environment, the effects have been limited and local. The generations now living are the first ones to have the knowledge and the technological power to consider controlling social evolution. What time scale to expect depends to a substantial extent on how soon we can bring population growth to a halt. In the United States we have already reached the stage of being able to produce all the goods we need; greater quantity is no longer a central problem. It is interesting to speculate on what life will be like when we cease trying to increase the quantity of everything, including people, and can devote our many talents to improving the quality of our occupations, our environment, and our lives—when we approach the mature or climax stage of civilization.

2. The Changing Demand for College Graduates

THERE has been much talk of manpower shortages in the past two decades—shortages of school teachers, faculty members, engineers, doctors, scientists, nurses, social workers, dentists, and other professionals and specialists. The cries of shortage have sometimes been exaggerated, and there has been some confusion between the number, say of nurses, that were needed and the number for which we have been willing to pay. But on the whole, college graduates and recipients of graduate and professional degrees have enjoyed a prolonged sellers' market. Beginning salaries have gone steadily upward, and many new graduates have had the excitement of being wooed by a number of prospective employers. Now the supply of college graduates and of new Ph.D.'s is catching up. Shortages will continue in some fields, but in others the sellers will not have things so much their own way. For the next few years the buyers can look forward to more choice than they have had in the 1950's and 1960's.[1]

As we move, quite suddenly, from a period of shortage to a period of supply sufficient to fill the demand in a number of specialized fields, college and university department chairmen who have for years been scrambling to fill faculty vacancies now find their desks covered with unsolicited applications. In September of 1969 the

[1] John K. Folger, Helen S. Astin, and Alan E. Bayer, *Human Resources and Higher Education*, Staff Report of the Commission on Human Resources and Advanced Education, New York, Russell Sage Foundation, 1970. Most of the data in this chapter are drawn from this report.

National Education Association announced that the teacher shortage in the United States had ended. There are still shortages in some localities and in some subjects, such as physics; and there are still teachers who have less than the standard qualifications; but in general, the teacher shortage has come to an end. In some other professions, such as engineering, demand still exceeds supply, and there are also fields, such as nursing and social work, in which we need more people than we are willing to pay adequately. But on the whole we are moving from a sellers' market to a buyers' market for college graduates. Students planning their careers and educational authorities planning college programs will have different options to consider and different problems to worry about than did their predecessors ten years ago.

The enrollment trends plotted in Figure 2 give a quick indication of the changes in some major supply relationships. As compared with the 1960's, enrollment in elementary and secondary schools will be almost stationary in the 1970's. College enrollment will increase, and graduate school enrollment will go up even more sharply. What the ten-year trend will be, however, is still uncertain. Index figures, rather than actual numbers, are plotted in this figure, for its purpose is to show how sharply the three enrollment trends are diverging.

In recent years, school teaching has constituted the largest single market for new college graduates. It took a third of all 1966 college graduates to fill the school teaching positions open that year. Now the stage of what seemed like ever-increasing school enrollment is past, and the U.S. Office of Education expects total ele-

Figure 2

Enrollment Trends, 1955-75 (1955=100%)

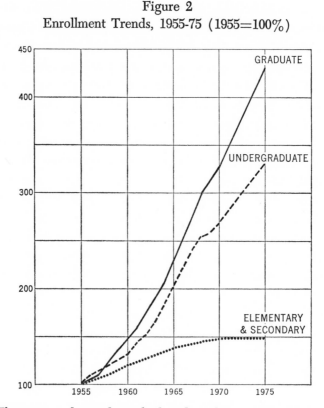

Elementary and secondary school, undergraduate, and graduate enrollments from 1955 to 1975, as percentages of 1955 enrollment. SOURCE: U.S. Office of Education.

mentary and secondary school enrollment to be only a little larger in 1980 than in 1970.[2] Birth rates have declined every year since 1957, and the number of babies born in 1968 was 800,000 fewer than the 4,300,000 born in the peak year of 1957. (However, since the babies

[2] Kenneth A. Simon and Marie G. Fullam, *Projections of Educational Statistics to 1977-78*, Washington, D.C., U.S. Office of Education, 1968.

of the postwar baby boom are coming of age, the number of marriages has already started to increase, the number of preschool children is likely to be substantially greater in 1980 than in 1970, and another rise in school enrollment can be expected.)

TABLE 1

Elementary and Secondary School Enrollment
in the United States, 1957-77

(in thousands)

Year (Fall)	Kindergarten Through Grade 8	Grades 9–12	Total
1957	29,530	8,621	38,151
1958	30,504	9,077	39,581
1959	31,511	9,271	40,782
1960	32,492	9,689	42,181
1961	32,895	10,469	43,364
1962	33,537	11,312	44,849
1963	34,304	12,183	46,487
1964	35,025	12,691	47,716
1965	34,463	13,010	48,473
1966	35,845	13,294	49,139
1967	36,240	13,647	49,887
PROJECTED			
1968	36,600	14,100	50,700
1969	36,600	14,500	51,200
1970	36,600	14,900	51,500
1971	36,300	15,300	51,700
1972	36,000	15,700	51,700
1973	35,700	16,000	51,700
1974	35,500	16,200	51,700
1975	35,300	16,500	51,700
1976	35,200	16,600	51,800
1977	35,300	16,600	51,900

Because each figure was rounded independently, the totals, from 1968 on, may not equal the sum of the K-8 and 9-12 figures. SOURCE: Simon and Fullam, *Projections of Educational Statistics to 1977-78*, table 2.

41

For the 1970's, school enrollment, as shown in Table 1, will not increase as rapidly as it did from 1950 until very recently. Consequently, the number of new teachers required will also fall off, and that fall has already begun. Instead of requiring a third of all new graduates as teachers, as was true in 1966, the schools will need only 22 percent of the 1970 graduates. In 1975 they will need only 17 percent, and in 1980 less than 15 percent. Even if the schools adopt a more favorable student-teacher ratio; if there are massive increases in kindergarten, Head Start, and other preschool opportunities; or if there are other changes that call for more teachers than are now projected, we will not within the foreseeable future need to use a third of all college graduates as school teachers. We may, on the contrary, have a large surplus of prospective teachers. At the end of 1969, the Commissioner of Labor Statistics told a congressional committee that if present trends continue, there will be 4.2 million prospective new teachers between 1968 and 1980 applying for the 2.4 million job openings of those years.[3]

Figure 2 also shows the changing relationship between the number of graduate students and undergraduate enrollment. College faculties are not the only employers of Ph.D.'s, but in some fields they almost reach that status. Over 90 percent of the Ph.D.'s in the arts and humanities are on college and university faculties. In engineering, by way of contrast, only 16 percent of the Ph.D.'s are so employed. Overall, about two

[3] *Higher Education and National Affairs*, Washington, D.C., American Council on Education, vol. 18, no. 44 (19 Dec. 1969): 4.

thirds of all new recipients of the doctor's degree either join or continue on college and university faculties. About 50 percent are employed primarily as teachers, and most of the other 16 percent are primarily engaged in research. College enrollments will continue to increase, but the peak rate of expansion now lies behind us. Faculties will have to keep on expanding, but not as many new faculty members will be needed in the next ten years as were needed in the past ten.

Saying that the supply is catching up with the demand does not mean that there will be widespread unemployment among college graduates or the holders of advanced degrees. Some of the new graduates will be unhappy; some will not get the jobs they most want; some will work at jobs they could have performed just as well without a college education; but they will be employed. There is so much flexibility in some parts of the employment market that employers can select applicants from a fairly wide range of quality and education. If lots of young college graduates are available, they get the jobs. If few graduates are available, the same jobs go to people with less education. This flexibility makes it almost meaningless to talk about the total demand for college graduates. We can count some kinds of jobs, such as teaching positions, for which a college diploma is required, but the countable positions requiring a college degree are only part of the total market. Because the rest of the market is so flexible, it is better to talk about the utilization of college graduates than to talk about the demand for them.

When they accept their first postcollege employment,

43

new graduates—either at the bachelor's level or at an advanced-degree level—can be thought of as being utilized in any of three ways. (1) Some replace previous workers who have retired, died, or moved to a different kind of work. (2) Some fill new positions that have been created because of the increased population or because of an expansion in some segment of the labor force. (3) And some raise the average educational level of the field they enter. If a college graduate goes to work for a bank, his job is of the first of these three types if he replaces an older college-graduate employee who has retired. His job is of the second type if he is part of an expanding staff of a new branch of the bank. And his job is of the third type if he fills a position that, had he not been available, would have gone to a high school graduate.

Although this third type of position may sound less attractive and perhaps even less respectable than the other two, it has been an important element in the changing pattern of employment for college graduates. High school graduates used to be considered sufficiently well educated to become elementary school teachers. Later, certification requirements were raised and it became necessary for the high school graduate to spend a couple of years at a normal school before he could begin teaching. Still later, there was further upgrading; a position that used to be filled by a normal school graduate now goes only to a person with a bachelor's degree. There is some argument as to whether or not school children are better taught than they used to be, but there is no uncertainty about the fact that for several decades many of the college graduates who became elementary teachers were replacing former teachers of lesser educational qualifications.

A comparable but less firmly institutionalized change has been going on in business. The business world has a voracious appetite for young men and women. Some of the jobs really do require the specialized knowledge that can most readily be acquired in a vocationally-oriented college curriculum. In many others, a college degree is not required, but if a college graduate is available, he gets the job.

Considering all employed college graduates in the United States in 1960, a majority were employed in fields in which most of their colleagues were not college graduates. Census records for 1960 show that 21 percent of the men and 16 percent of the women with degrees were in fields in which 90 percent or more of all workers were college graduates, for example, law or high school teaching; 24 percent of the men and 45 percent of the women were in fields in which a majority of workers had college degrees, for example, engineering or the ministry; the other 55 percent of the men and 39 percent of the women graduates were in fields in which college graduates were minorities.

Widespread flexibility in employment standards and the opportunity for educational upgrading in some fields mean that the larger supply of graduates we can now anticipate will be utilized. Many new employees will be better educated than their predecessors, and sometimes that will mean that they can work more productively than their predecessors. But sometimes it will merely mean that employers will have raised their entrance requirements, thus taking practical advantage of the larger supply of graduates by using college graduation as an applicant-screening device.

The Market for College Graduates in the 1970's

For the past twenty years, as shown in Figure 3, the number of men graduating from college has been great-

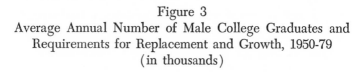

Figure 3
Average Annual Number of Male College Graduates and Requirements for Replacement and Growth, 1950-79
(in thousands)

Comparison of average annual numbers of male college graduates from 1950-59 to 1975-79 with the numbers required to replace former employees who had college degrees and to expand the labor force without changing the graduate-nongraduate ratio. SOURCE: Folger, Astin, and Bayer, *Human Resources and Higher Education*

er than the number necessary to replace retiring college graduates and to expand the labor force. The excess has gone into sales, marketing, other business activities, and still other fields in which college education has sometimes been helpful and sometimes has merely given the graduate an edge over less educated competitors. During the 1950's, about a third of the male college graduates were available for positions of this third type. During the 1960's, the economy grew more rapidly and there was a smaller surplus of men graduating from college. In the 1970's, however, there will again be a substantial number available for the educational upgrading of the fields they enter.

Figure 4 presents comparable data for female graduates. When account is taken of the fact that about 20 percent of the women graduating from college do not enter the labor force, the number of female graduates has been much closer to the number needed for replacement and expansion than has been true of male graduates. During the 1950's, only about a tenth of the female graduates were available to raise the educational level of the fields they entered. During the 1960's, there was no excess of this kind. But in the 1970's, there will again be enough female graduates to raise the average educational level of the fields they enter.

This kind of educational upgrading sometimes takes place much more slowly and painfully than it does in the United States. In some countries the holder of a university degree considers it quite beneath his dignity to enter some kinds of work. If he cannot find a position for which his university degree presumably prepared him, he would rather remain unemployed than take a

47

Figure 4

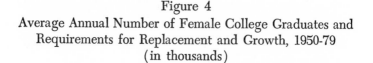

Average Annual Number of Female College Graduates and
Requirements for Replacement and Growth, 1950-79
(in thousands)

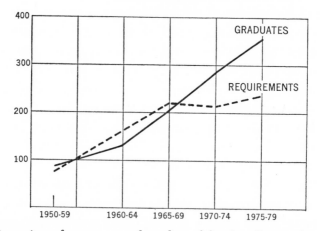

Comparison of average annual numbers of female college graduates
from 1950-59 to 1975-79 with the numbers required to replace former
employees who had college degrees and to expand the labor force
without changing the graduate-nongraduate ratio. The number of
graduates plotted has been reduced to 80 percent of the actual number
of women receiving degrees to make an approximate adjustment for
the women who do not enter the labor force at the time of college
graduation. SOURCE: Folger, Astin, and Bayer, *Human Resources and
Higher Education*

job beneath his status. Sadly, in a number of countries,
many young graduates have not found work to their
liking. India provides a striking contrast with the United
States in this respect. Unemployment in the United
States is concentrated among the least well educated.
In India, unemployment is highest among persons with
the most education. At the time of the last Indian census, 16 percent of all recent science and engineering
graduates were unemployed, and an additional 40 per-

48

cent, although employed, were not working in the fields of their training. Since that census, the ranks of the unemployed are reported to have been swelling by 14,000 new graduates a year. In the Philippines, a third of the medical school graduates never even start to practice medicine. In Burma, 40 percent of the engineering graduates in the class of 1961 had not found engineering positions within a year and a half after receiving their degrees.[4]

These unhappy figures are by no means all that is involved in explaining the wish to migrate to the United States or Europe where jobs are more plentiful, but they explain a lot of the so-called brain drain. The United States has been blessedly free of rigid attitudes about what kind of employment is suitable for a college graduate. Some jobs carry higher prestige than others; some pay better; some have other advantages, but the typical college graduate has thought it better to accept the best job available than to be out of work. For their part, employers have usually wanted to employ the best-qualified applicant they could find, and that has often been interpreted to mean the one with the most education. Thus there have regularly been jobs for college graduates, and the concept of a surplus of college graduates has had little meaning. Nor do I anticipate an overall surplus in the 1970's. There will be enough new graduates for the jobs that require college degrees, and the rest of the graduates will be employed in work for which a college degree is optional but not required.

4 Walter Adams, ed., *The Brain Drain*, New York, Macmillan Co., 1968. This volume includes a variety of information about the ability, or inability, of a number of countries to make effective use of their university graduates.

The Markets in Selected Fields

So much for college graduates as a group. When we look at individual fields, it becomes more difficult to give numerical estimates, for there is enough changing of college majors and enough shifting among different kinds of work to make numerical predictions quite unreliable. But in general, the analyses of the Commission on Human Resources and Advanced Education indicate the following relationships.

School Teaching. As pointed out earlier, it is clear that school teaching will not require as large a fraction of the college graduating classes as in the recent past. This situation offers the country some options. If there should be an effective move toward substantial increases in kindergarten, Head Start, or other preschool programs, enough teachers will be available.

This new situation will also require school administrators to do some thinking about how they can best select new teachers. When a choice is available, it is customary to choose the applicant with the best college record. But if this is the basis for selecting new school teachers, the results may not be altogether happy. Typically, women who prepare to be teachers earn better college grades than do men who plan on teaching. Selecting on the basis of grades when many candidates are available would mean selecting more women and fewer men. Moreover, the men who make the best grades in college are precisely the ones who are most likely to leave teaching after a year or two to enter other kinds of work. Selecting on the basis of college grades would therefore run counter to the social and psychological judgment that it would be good for the students to have more men teachers. Ideally, selection would be on the basis of whatever traits make for excellent teaching, but there is little evidence that anyone can do a particularly good job of identifying those traits or of selecting the applicants who possess them.

Engineering. The demand for engineers is increasing by about 50,000 a year, and close to 15,000 a year are needed to replace losses. Schools of engineering are now graduating fewer than 45,000 a year, and it is quite unlikely that they will graduate enough engineers to meet the demand of the coming five to ten years. Engineering, unlike most of the other large professions, has not been rigid about its entrance requirements. In the past, graduates with engineering degrees, college dropouts who started in engineering school but did not run the full course, college graduates with degrees in other fields, technicians, and persons with no college education at all but with appropriate experience have all come to be classed as engineers. In the 1960 census, 56 percent of the engineers had college degrees, 19 percent had some college work, and 25 percent had not attended college at all. Census reports for 1940 and 1950 showed roughly comparable figures. Since 1960, the percentage of engineers with college degrees has been edging upward and is probably now at about the 60 percent level, but this is still a long way from 100 percent. During the 1970's, we can expect engineering jobs to be available for all new engineering graduates, and we can also expect that many men will move into professional engineering work who are not graduates in engineering.

Nursing. Nursing is the second largest profession for women and has been the one with the lowest pay.

Nurses' salaries are below those of school teachers, social workers, librarians, and employees in other fields that hire large numbers of women, and most of these other professions offer shorter or more regular hours of work and, in some respects, more attractive working conditions. As a result, growth in the supply of nurses has been slow; nursing is becoming less popular as a career choice for young women; and much of the demand of recent years has been met by drawing older nurses back into practice and by employing less well-trained practical nurses.

There is some possibility that the shortage may be eased by a spillover of young women who at other times would have entered school teaching, and Medicare and Medicaid programs are helping to force hospitals to raise nursing salaries. Even so, nursing is likely to continue to be a shortage field.

Social Welfare Work. This is a profession with such fuzzy boundaries that it is hard to measure either supply or demand. Most positions are filled by persons who lack professional qualifications in social work, and most who do gain professional qualifications (e.g., the master's degree in social work) do so only after they have begun to work in the field.

Salaries are low; turnover is rapid; and employers are beset by constant difficulties in finding enough social welfare workers. Again there is some possibility of an easing of the situation because of lessened opportunities in teaching, but like nursing, the situation will probably continue to be unsatisfactory unless some miracle brings higher salaries or higher status to the field.

Law. There is no easy and natural basis for projecting

the future demand for lawyers, in the way that the number of students can be used for predicting the demand for teachers. One can project the number of lawyers on the basis of the total population, if he believes that the demand is based on the number of people who might need legal services. Or one can project on the basis of the expected Gross National Product, if he thinks it is the number of dollars rather than the number of people that determines the demand for legal services. Or, as a third alternative, one can base his projections on the increasing complexity of the nation's social and economic problems.

Projecting on any of these bases, or projecting on the number of students who are likely to be interested in becoming lawyers, will result in numbers greater than the expected capacity of the nation's schools of law. Unless law schools expand their enrollment or unless new law schools are established more rapidly than now seems likely, there is little danger of having a surplus of lawyers in the next decade.

Medicine. The number of applicants for admission to medical schools is increasing and the average quality of those admitted is on the rise. If the medical schools had the capacity, the number of physicians could increase substantially faster than anyone expects it actually will, and could do so without loss of quality. The actual growth will be controlled by the capacity of the medical schools and is expected to keep pace with the population growth. As in the past, there will also be an inflow of graduates of foreign medical schools who come to this country for internship and residency training. Altogether, it is expected that the current ratio of

53

about 164 physicians to each 100,000 of population will be maintained.

Business and Commerce. The Commission on Human Resources and Advanced Education made no effort to project either supply or demand figures for business and commerce. Numerical requirements are so great and employment standards are so flexible that this area provides a very expansible or contractable job market for college graduates.

The Market for Ph.D.'s

The nation's graduate schools are conferring Ph.D. degrees at a rate no one would have predicted fifteen or twenty years ago. The number has gone up because in a period of long-sustained economic and educational expansion, industry, government agencies, and academic institutions have had a large appetite for young Ph.D.'s; because the federal government has provided many graduate fellowships and traineeships and much money for the employment of research assistants; and because there has been a ready supply of able students eager to take advantage of the opportunities these conditions presented.

The resulting numbers of Ph.D. degrees conferred or expected to be conferred from 1920 to 1978 are shown in Figure 5. The years beyond 1969 are projections, but many of the candidates for those years are already in graduate school, and the actual numbers up through 1975 will probably not differ greatly from the numbers projected. After 1974 or 1975 the projection is more uncertain. At some time in the not too distant future the rate of increase will have to slow down. The long-run

54

Figure 5
Ph.D. Degrees Conferred in the United States, 1920-78

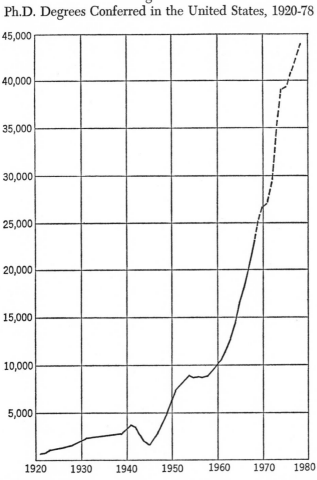

SOURCE: Folger, Astin, and Bayer, *Human Resources and Higher Education.*

trend in Ph.D. degrees will continue upward, but less steeply than at present. Support for graduate students is not increasing as rapidly as it was, and positions for new Ph.D.'s are not opening up in as large numbers as

55

they were through most of the 1960's. In response to these conditions, some of the larger universities have decreased the numbers of new graduate students admitted. Other universities, however, including many of the less prestigious and less well-established ones, are still seeking to expand their graduate enrollment.

The end of the 1960's was the end of a long period—long in the memories of graduate students—in which jobs were more plentiful than new Ph.D.'s. In 1969, letters to the editors of some of the professional journals began to complain of the lack of jobs. Termination of government contracts threw a few industrial scientists out of work, some of whom complained bitterly about the continuation of graduate fellowship programs when they and other older workers were seeking employment.

A survey by *Physics Today* of 1968 recipients of Ph.D. degrees in physics reported that in the summer of that year, 30 percent had not yet received a single firm job offer. A resurvey in the fall of 1968 showed almost all of this group to have been placed, but quite a few had jobs only because they were retained by the universities which had conferred their degrees.[5]

Each year at the spring and fall meetings of the American Chemical Society, a placement service is provided at which chemists seeking jobs and employers seeking chemists can be brought together. In the decade ending with 1967, there were always fewer applicants than employers at the fall meetings of the ACS, with average registrations of 476 applicants and 900 employers. In 1968, the 604 applicants closely balanced

[5] Susanne D. Ellis, "The Graduate Student: Where Does He Come From? Where Does He Go?" *Physics Today*, vol. 22, no. 3 (1969): 53-57.

the 620 employers, but at the fall meeting of 1969, there were 880 applicants and only 481 employers.

Other professional societies conduct similar placement services, or "slave markets." At meetings held during Christmas week of 1969, the placement services of the American Historical Association and the Modern Language Association both provided newspaper stories about anxious young scholars looking unsuccessfully for jobs. At the American Historical Association meeting, more than 2,000 young historians—twice the number of the year before—competed for the openings listed by 225 colleges. Young scholars in English and foreign languages encountered equally discouraging prospects at the annual meeting of the Modern Language Association.

These reports from the 1969 annual meetings in chemistry, history, and languages are far from being the whole story, for many appointments are arranged through channels other than annual placement services. Nevertheless, if one wants to know what the job prospects will be for new Ph.D.'s, college and university faculty openings constitute the best single indicator. College enrollment will keep on going up, and faculties will keep on expanding, but undergraduate enrollment is not expected to climb quite as rapidly in the years ahead as it has been climbing recently (see Table 2), and the projections of the Commission on Human Resources and Advanced Education indicate that it will not be necessary to employ as many new college teachers in 1971-75 as were needed in 1966-70.

Figure 6 compares the number of Ph.D. degrees conferred with the number of new college teachers required

TABLE 2

Enrollment in Institutions of Higher Education, 1957-77

(in thousands)

Year	Under-graduates Enrolled for Degree Credit	Graduate Students Enrolled for Degree Credit	Total Including Students Not Enrolled for Degree Credit
1957	2,760	288	3,224
1958	2,924	312	3,420
1959	3,046	331	3,571
1960	3,227	356	3,789
1961	3,474	386	4,047
1962	3,753	422	4,404
1963	4,031	464	4,766
1964	4,433	517	5,280
1965	4,945	582	5,921
1966	5,261	624	6,390
1967	5,659	688	6,912
PROJECTED			
1968	6,010	749	7,369
1969	6,125	781	7,541
1970	6,353	828	7,852
1971	6,644	886	8,243
1972	6,974	952	8,686
1973	7,303	1,019	9,130
1974	7,609	1,085	9,549
1975	7,904	1,152	9,956
1976	8,171	1,217	10,332
1977	8,405	1,279	10,667

Column 1 includes students in 2-year or 4-year institutions who are enrolled in programs that give credit toward a bachelor's degree or a first professional degree such as M.D., D.D.S., D.V.M., LL.B., or B.D. Column 2 includes graduate students who are beyond the bachelor's or first professional-degree level. They may or may not be working toward an advanced degree. Column 3 includes students in columns 1 and 2 plus others who are in programs, such as vocational or general-studies programs, that cannot be used as credit toward a degree. SOURCE: Simon and Fullam, *Projections of Educational Statistics to 1977-78*, tables 4, 12, and 13.

each year from 1959 through 1978. Graduate assistants, who by definition do not yet have the doctorate, and teachers in non-degree programs, who rarely hold the doctorate, are not included in the count of new teachers required. Through most of the 1960's, there would not have been enough new Ph.D.'s to meet the new teaching needs even if all had gone into teaching and none into industrial or other positions. Through the 1970's, the number of new Ph.D.'s will be much greater than the number of new teachers required. The sellers' market of the 1950's and 1960's will be a buyers' market in the 1970's.

Table 3 gives U.S. Office of Education projections of Ph.D. degrees granted and expected to be granted in four broad areas through 1978. The Commission on Human Resources and Advanced Education has compared the numbers of doctorates conferred in these four areas with the numbers of new college and university teachers needed in each. The four areas are: the physical sciences, mathematics, and engineering; the biological sciences; the social sciences, including psychology; and the arts and humanities. Figures 7, 8, 9, and 10, which are all constructed in the same way, compare the numbers of new Ph.D. degrees granted or expected to be granted with the numbers of new faculty members required in each of several five-year periods. The numbers of degrees shown are totals, exclusive of foreign students who did not or are not expected to remain in the United States, regardless of the kind of job the person took or is expected to take. The job requirements shown are only for teaching faculty positions at four-year institutions. The figures do not show total

Figure 6
Ph.D. Degrees Conferred and Requirements for Replacement and Growth of College and University Faculties, 1959-78

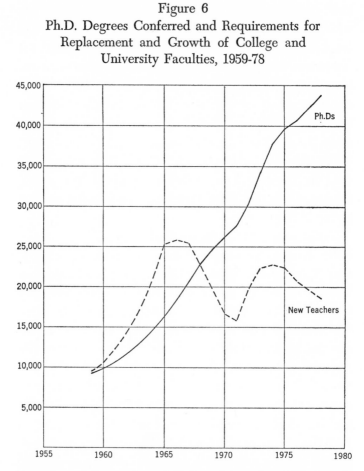

Comparison of the numbers of Ph.D. recipients from 1959 through 1978 with the numbers of new college and university teachers required for replacement and expansion during those years. (The requirement figures do not include graduate teaching assistants or teachers in programs that do not lead to a college degree.) SOURCE: Simon and Fullam, *Projections of Educational Statistics to 1977-78*, Ph.D.'s from table 22, new teachers from table 29 (with replacement at 2 percent a year), 3-year moving averages.

TABLE 3

Ph.D. Degrees Conferred in Selected Fields,
1957-58 to 1977-78

	Mathematics, Physical Sciences, and Engineering	Biological Sciences	Arts and Humanities	Psychology and Social Sciences
1957-58	2,549	1,625	1,073	1,716
1958-59	2,808	1,586	1,188	1,843
1959-60	2,927	1,768	1,250	1,923
1960-61	3,278	1,789	1,345	2,072
1961-62	3,725	1,958	1,430	2,172
1962-63	4,248	2,074	1,538	2,401
1963-64	4,744	2,390	1,753	2,742
1964-65	5,641	2,658	1,991	3,031
1965-66	6,150	2,966	2,180	3,361
1966-67	6,830	3,180	2,370	3,630
1967-68	7,810	3,510	2,640	4,040
1968-69	9,000	3,910	2,970	4,520
1969-70	9,690	4,070	3,120	4,740
1970-71	10,060	4,070	3,160	4,780
1971-72	11,080	4,340	3,410	5,130
1972-73	13,540	5,110	4,070	6,100
1973-74	15,360	5,610	4,510	6,750
1974-75	15,800	5,570	4,530	6,770
1975-76	16,590	5,660	4,670	6,920
1976-77	17,300	5,800	4,910	7,130
1977-78	18,240	6,030	5,020	7,430

SOURCE: Simon and Fullam, *Projections of Educational Statistics to 1977-78*, table 22.

faculty size, but rather the number of new college teachers needed to replace retiring teachers and to provide for increased enrollment. Moreover, the requirements are for teaching duties only; research appointments and the equivalent of time spent on research by faculty members who divide their time between teaching and research are not included.

61

In the physical sciences, mathematics, and engineering (Figure 7), about 40 percent of all Ph.D.'s in the country are employed on university and college faculties for teaching or research, with 25 to 30 percent in teaching positions. From 1955 through 1965, the faculties of the country were expanding rapidly and for teaching duties alone could have absorbed about 70 percent of the new Ph.D.'s in the physical sciences. They did not get that many, however, for industry and government took a considerable number. Because there were not enough Ph.D.'s to fill the faculty vacancies, many of those positions were filled by persons without the doctorate. In the past five years, 1965 to 1970, the college demands equaled about half of the total number of new degrees. In the five years ahead, colleges and universities will need approximately a quarter of the number of new degree recipients as teachers. There will therefore be a larger percentage as well as a larger number available for other kinds of appointments.

In the biological sciences (Figure 8), 55 percent of all Ph.D.'s are found on faculties, and 35 percent are primarily teachers. Some biologists with doctor's degrees are employed in government, industry, or elsewhere outside the academic world, but the percentage is smaller than it is for physical scientists. For the past fifteen years the number of new doctor's degrees in the biological sciences has been slightly larger than the number that were wanted for faculty teaching appointments. Not all took faculty positions, however, and as a result colleges and universities had to appoint many teachers with lesser degree qualifications. In the five years ahead, there will be enough new Ph.D.'s in biology

Figure 7
New Teaching Faculty Required and New Ph.D.'s in
Engineering, Mathematics, and the Physical Sciences,
1955-75

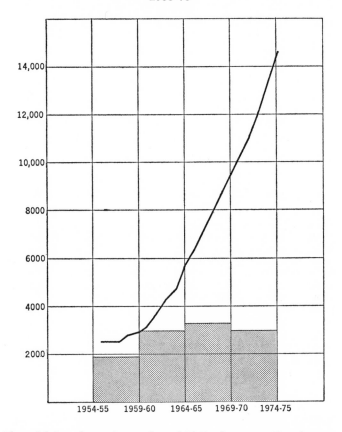

The solid line shows the number of Ph.D. degrees conferred or expected to be conferred in engineering, mathematics, and the physical
sciences. The shaded area shows the number of new college and
university teachers required in these fields. Foreign students who
return to their own countries are not included in the Ph.D. curve.
The requirements shown are for teaching in 4-year colleges and
universities. Junior college faculty and research positions are not
included. SOURCE: Folger, Astin, and Bayer, *Human Resources and
Higher Education*

Figure 8
New Teaching Faculty Required and New Ph.D.'s in the
Biological Sciences, 1955-75

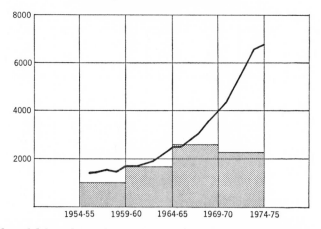

The solid line shows the number of Ph.D. degrees conferred or expected to be conferred in the biological sciences. The shaded area
shows the number of new college and university teachers required in
these fields. Foreign students who return to their own countries are
not included in the Ph.D. curve. The requirements shown are for
teaching in 4-year colleges and universities. Junior college faculty and
research positions are not included. SOURCE: Folger, Astin, and Bayer,
Human Resources and Higher Education

to fill all the new college vacancies and about 14,000
more available for other kinds of positions.

Sixty percent of social scientists are employed on
faculties, 42 percent as teachers and 18 percent in research. Faculty demands have been growing more
rapidly in the social sciences than in the physical or
biological sciences, and consequently the colleges and
universities have needed to make substantially more
new appointments in the social sciences, especially in the
five years now ending. As Figure 9 shows, there have not
been enough new Ph.D.'s in the social sciences to meet

64

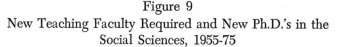

Figure 9
New Teaching Faculty Required and New Ph.D.'s in the
Social Sciences, 1955-75

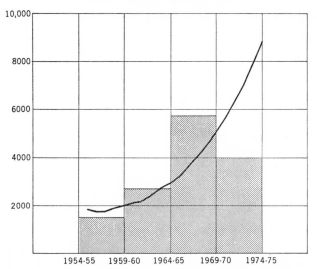

The solid line shows the number of Ph.D. degrees conferred or expected to be conferred in psychology and the social sciences. The
shaded area shows the number of new college and university teachers
required in these fields. Foreign students who return to their own
countries are not included in the Ph.D. curve. The requirements shown
are for teaching in 4-year colleges and universities. Junior college
faculty and research positions are not included. SOURCE: Folger, Astin,
and Bayer, *Human Resources and Higher Education*

faculty needs, let alone provide any new appointees for
other sectors, but that too is changing. In the five years
ahead, there will be enough Ph.D.'s in the social sciences
to fill all new faculty posts and to provide about 14,000
for other kinds of positions.

Figure 10 shows where the real shortage is to be
found, in the arts and humanities. Over 90 percent of the
recipients of Ph.D. degrees in these fields are employed
on faculties, almost all of them as teachers. In the past

65

fifteen years, there have not been nearly enough to meet faculty needs. Nor will the number of new doctor's degrees conferred in these fields in the next five years be sufficient to match campus requirements for new faculty members. (See note to Figure 10.)

Another way to state the sharp transition in the relation between the supply of new Ph.D.'s and the demands for new college professors is to bring the figures down to the level of the individual holder of a brand-new doctor's degree. In the physical sciences, there has been, in the five years ending with 1970, about .60 college

Figure 10
New Teaching Faculty Required and New Ph.D.'s in the Arts and Humanities, 1955-75

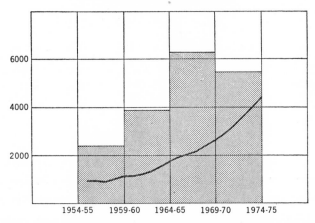

Note added in press: This figure is similar to Figures 7, 8, and 9, but since it was prepared, prospects for new Ph.D.'s in the arts and humanities have become less favorable. Financial difficulties of colleges and universities plus the fact that a number of institutions no longer require undergraduate students to study a foreign language have reduced the number of openings, especially in modern foreign languages, to considerably fewer than were expected when the figure and text were prepared.

66

teaching job for each new physical science Ph.D. In the five years beginning with 1970, there will be about .37 college teaching job for each new Ph.D. In the biological sciences, the change is from 1.00 job per new Ph.D. to .45 job per Ph.D. The comparable change in the social sciences is from 1.50 jobs to .60 job. Students who earn the doctorate in the arts and humanities and who want academic appointments will also have to search harder. Their ratio will change from 3.00 jobs per new Ph.D. to 1.50 jobs per new Ph.D.

There is no comparably simple way to show the number of new Ph.D.'s likely to be needed for research and other kinds of work, for it is more difficult to forecast the numbers of research positions that are likely to open up. Much depends upon the rate of increase in funds for research and development. Funds for that purpose rose very rapidly for a dozen years beginning about 1953, but since 1966 the rate of increase has been very much smaller, and if one takes account of inflation, research and development funds have actually declined since 1966. We can expect increases in the future, but not the rapid increases of the past.

With respect to new recipients of the doctor's degree, we are therefore in about the same state described earlier for new college graduates. If we were justified in talking of shortages in the past, we had better speak of surpluses now, but again this does not mean unemployment. People with doctoral degrees will be employed, but society will utilize them in somewhat different and broader ways than in the past.

In 1960, about 60 percent of the teaching faculty of four-year colleges and universities held doctor's degrees.

67

Now, in making new appointments, the colleges and universities have an opportunity to move toward a higher Ph.D. ratio. Other kinds of employers will have a similar opportunity. Junior colleges have been employing only 2 or 3 percent of the new Ph.D.'s. They can now look forward to employing more if they wish. Research and development laboratories and other industrial and governmental employers will also have opportunities to increase the percentage of Ph.D.'s on their staffs in the decade ahead. It is worth noting in passing that these trends will put a squeeze on those with only a master's degree. Recipients of that degree will not fare as well as they did when Ph.D.'s were in short supply.

Longer Range Trends

Looking farther into the future, an expanded demand must be expected. It is too optimistic to expect that population growth will be stopped by 1980; an increasing population will need more people in all the specialized fields. Elementary school enrollment—approximately stable during the 1970's—will be on the rise as the young adults born in the baby boom of the 1950's send their children to school. The Gross National Product for 1980, as tentatively forecast now, may be 50 percent, or $500 billion, higher than in 1970. All of these expectations indicate that demand in the professions and specialized fields will increase substantially.

Manpower projections for the ten years ahead cannot be taken as precise predictions of the relations between supply and demand that will exist at that time. They do, however, indicate the direction and the approximate rate of change, and thus serve as useful guides for planning.[6] Projections by the National Science Foundation[7] of the relations between the total number of Ph.D.'s to be expected in science and engineering in 1980 and the total demand for science and engineering Ph.D.'s at that time can be used as one such guide. The total supply of employed Ph.D.'s in science and engineering in the United States in January 1968 was estimated to be 147,000. This number, less those who die or leave the labor force, plus new graduates and new immigrants, is expected to increase to 350,000 in 1980.

Three methods were used to project the 1980 demand. The first two methods assumed reasonable growth trends in academic requirements, federal and industrial research funds, and other variables associated with the demand for Ph.D.'s. These two methods gave 1980 demand totals of 277,000 and 301,000, both figures substantially below the projected supply of 350,000. But both these methods, the authors thought, might be too cautious. Research and development funds might grow more rapidly than the GNP; the percentage of faculty members holding Ph.D. degrees might increase more rapidly than assumed in the other projections; and the number of Ph.D.'s engaged in activities other than teaching and research might expand more rapidly in the future. If all of these things happen, the total demand might reach 380,000 or 390,000 in 1980, figures somewhat above the anticipated supply of 350,000.

But the authors may have been too optimistic; research and development funds have not been increasing

[6] Dael Wolfle, *Can Professional Manpower Trends Be Predicted?* Washington, D.C., U.S. Department of Labor, 1967.

[7] National Science Foundation, *Science and Engineering Doctorate Supply and Utilization, 1968-80*, NSF 69-37, Washington, D.C., U.S. Government Printing Office, 1969.

as rapidly as they hoped. Moreover, universities continue to expand their graduate programs, and expect to grant perhaps 60,000 Ph.D.'s in 1980. The inertia inherent in the system, the fact that most of the recipients of Ph.D. degrees in the middle 1970's are already in graduate school, and the ambitions of many universities to gain the greater prestige that comes with larger graduate enrollment all combine to indicate that there will be substantially more new Ph.D.'s in the 1970's than will be needed in the kinds of positions for which the doctorate has traditionally been required. A substantial number will have to find other kinds of positions.

Conclusions

One can draw several conclusions from the trends described in this chapter. The flexibility of employment standards indicates that college graduates and recipients of advanced degrees will almost all find employment. Nevertheless, some significant changes must be expected.

Some men and women coming from colleges and universities will have a harder time finding the jobs they want than have the graduates of the past decade. Some may be unemployed for a while.

The sharp decline in the percentage of college graduates needed as elementary and secondary school teachers will make a large number of graduates available for other kinds of work, and should, of course, influence the distribution of majors selected by undergraduate students.

Colleges and universities can exercise more choice in the selection of new faculty members, and other employers of persons with the Ph.D. degree will also have a larger supply from which to choose.

It may be tempting to respond to these projections by reducing funds for higher education, or by restricting college and graduate enrollment. To do so would constitute a major change in social policy. If we give way to pessimism, we are likely to lay the basis for other difficulties in later years. We have not in the past followed the policy of trying to match the number of graduates with estimated future requirements. We should not now try to reduce future graduation rates just because, for the time being, we seem to have quite an ample supply. It may be desirable to restrict the numbers of new Ph.D.'s in the decade ahead, but before instituting such a program it will surely be desirable to plan utilization levels better than we ever have in the past. Those plans will have to take account of the numbers needed for college teaching and other traditional forms of employment and also of decisions concerning the attainment of the national goals discussed in Chapter Six.

3. The Return on Educational Investments

COLLEGES and universities now spend over $20 billion a year for educational activities, but that is not the total cost of higher education. Students also have books and supplies to purchase, and the more than half of them who live away from home have living and travel expenses to meet. Moreover, all students forego the money they would be earning if they were not in college. Expenses paid by students, the additional educational expenses paid for by taxes, gifts, or earnings on endowment, plus foregone earnings for the 7.5 million students now in American colleges and universities must total upwards of $75 billion a year, or $10,000 per student per year.

Do the graduates get their money's worth? Does society get its money's worth? It has long been known that college graduates have higher incomes than nongraduates. The difference is partly explained by the fact that college degrees, as well as graduate and professional degrees, provide entrée into medicine, law, dentistry, and some of the other higher paying professions that are not open to people with less education. Even those college graduates who do enter the same kinds of work as nongraduates tend to earn more than their fellow workers.

Society, too, appears to profit. From 1897 through 1957, the economic output of the United States increased at an average rate of 3.5 percent a year. Edward Denison,[1] in a detailed analysis of the factors involved

[1] Edward F. Denison, "Measuring the Contribution of Education (and the Residual) to Economic Growth," in *The Residual Factor and*

72

in this steady increase, concluded that a little more than half of the annual growth was due to larger inputs of capital and labor. The amount of wealth devoted to commerce and industry increased substantially between 1897 and 1957, and the number of workers also increased, but both increases together accounted for only a little over half of the 3.5 percent a year increase in production. The rest of the annual increase—the "residual factor" as it has been called—Dr. Denison attributed to a more highly educated working force, new knowledge, and the better management and organization that education and new knowledge made possible.

Other economists have used somewhat different methods of analyzing the economic benefits of education. Theodore Schultz of the University of Chicago first gave prominence to a new kind of economic analysis in his 1960 presidential address to the American Economic Association, an address he called "Investment in Human Capital."[2] Schultz and several other economists have calculated the economic value of education in essentially the same way they would calculate the value of other kinds of investments, by determining the annual rate of return on the initial investment. The higher lifetime earnings of college graduates, in comparison with nongraduates, can be considered as a return—or divi-

---

Economic Growth, Paris, Organization for Economic Co-operation and Development, 1964.

[2] Theodore W. Schultz, "Investment in Human Capital," The American Economic Review, 51 (1961): 1-17. Another pioneer and excellent source is Gary S. Becker, Human Capital, New York, Columbia University Press (for the National Bureau of Economic Research), 1964. A useful collection of papers on the topic of investment in education is Mark Blaug's Economics of Education, vol. 1, Baltimore, Penguin Books (Penguin Education X56), 1968.

dend—on the costs of going to college, including the earnings foregone during the college years.

Analyses of this kind show rather consistently that the average college graduate enjoys an annual return of 12 to 15 percent on the costs of his education. Of course there is variation about this average. Some graduates enjoy a high rate of return, as much as 25 percent a year or more; others may not get any return. The variation among professions is not as large as one might expect. Physicians generally have higher incomes than members of other professional groups, but medical education is very costly, and it turns out that physicians, engineers, dentists, and even school teachers are closer together in the rates of return on the costs of their education than in the absolute values of their average annual earnings. Lee Hansen, in analyzing such differences, has suggested that changes or differences in the rate of return can be used as a sensitive measure of supply-demand relationships.[3]

There is a satisfying quality about these findings. Money invested in education should pay a return in some form, and it is appropriate to ask how the return compares with the cost. Higher earnings do not constitute the only value of education, but potential economic benefit is a common and legitimate reason for going to college. In the *Wealth of Nations*, Adam Smith wrote: "A man educated at the expense of much labour and time to any of those employments which require extraordinary dexterity and skill . . . [should receive wages] over and above the usual wages of common labour

[3] W. Lee Hansen, "The Economics of Scientific and Engineering Manpower," *The Journal of Human Resources*, vol. 2, no. 2 (1967): 191-215.

[that] will replace to him the whole expense of his education, with at least the ordinary profits of an equally valuable capital."[4]

It is appropriate to ask how the rate of return on money invested in education compares with the return that might be obtained from other investments, and 12 to 15 percent a year seems quite satisfactory as an alternative to investing in real estate or the stock market.

Studies of the rate of return have been conducted over a long enough period so that it is possible to make some temporal comparisons. Figure 11 shows the average rates of return on the costs of high school and college education at several periods from 1939 to 1961.[5] At the high school level there has been a consistent upward trend. High school graduates have been getting a larger and larger return on the costs of their education. In fact, the rate of return doubled between 1939 and 1961. At the college level, there seemed to be a slight decline between 1939 and the late 1950's, but a subsequent rise brought the curve back up again. Perhaps the prudent generalization is that there has been no evidence of a major change in the 1939-61 period. When 1970 census data become available, it will be possible to determine what the rate of return was in 1969.

Studies similar to those conducted in the United States have been carried out in England, France, Israel, India, and several of the Latin American countries. Educational costs, economic conditions, salaries, and rates of return on educational costs vary widely among

[4] Adam Smith, *Wealth of Nations*, book I, part I, chapter X.
[5] Becker, *Human Capital*.

75

Figure 11
Private Rates of Return on the Costs of High School
and College Education, 1939-61

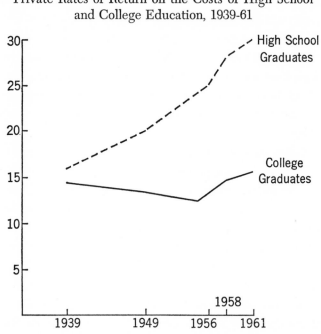

These rates include foregone earnings. SOURCE: Becker, *Human Capital.*

these countries. Comparing the rates of return with the economic conditions leads to the important generalization that the rate of return on the costs of education depends very much upon the rate of capital formation—or the rate of economic development—of the country. In a sense, this conclusion is nothing more than an elaborate way of stating the obvious fact that if a college graduate is to earn a good rate of return on the costs of his education, there must be a job with a good salary for him to step into. In countries which cannot employ their graduates effectively, the rate of return on educa-

76

tional costs is low. In India, for example, the rate is much lower than in the United States because there are not enough suitable jobs for university graduates in India.

Even though it may be obvious that education is not a good investment unless there are suitable jobs for graduates, the fact is nevertheless worth stating. Education has sometimes been treated as if it stood alone, independent of the rest of society and the economy. Sometimes education has also been expanded as if, almost by itself, it constituted the key to economic advancement, but it is not, as some of the developing countries are learning. If a country expects a good rate of return on the money invested in education, the rate of investment in education must be kept in balance with the rate of investment in physical capital.

In the United States, college graduates have continued to receive a good rate of return on the costs of higher education because the money spent on it has been in sufficiently good balance with the money devoted to expanding the economy, and thus to creating suitable positions for millions of college graduates. But if the rate at which new graduates leave the university should begin to run too far ahead of the rate of economic development, the return on educational investments would begin to turn downward. It has not happened yet, but that is no guarantee against a downturn in the future.

An annual return of 12 to 15 percent is a good return; it has held up for several decades; it compares favorably with the return on other ways of investing capital. Nevertheless, the figure must be treated with much

77

caution, for in one sense it underestimates the true return, and in another sense it overestimates the return.

Consider first the underestimate. Students go to college for a variety of reasons: some to prepare themselves to enter one of the professions, some to get away from home, some to have a good time, some to learn, some to widen their range of friends and acquaintances, others for still different reasons, and many for more than one reason. These are all honest objectives, and in considering the economics of education, it would be proper to charge part of the cost to each kind of reason. If students get enjoyment or other immediate rewards out of going to college, some of the cost can properly be considered as an immediate consumption expense. If a student acquires an understanding and appreciation of physics or Shakespeare or French history, of music, the graphic arts, or the differences among the great religions of the world, he has surely gained from his years in college even if the gain does not result in increased earnings. But deciding how the total cost should be allocated among the different reasons would be pretty much a guessing game, and the proper fractions would surely differ widely for different students. To avoid such guesses in calculating the rate of return, all costs of education have been treated as investments intended to augment future earnings. Thus if one could take account of the fact that students gain several kinds of benefits from college attendance, the rate of return on that portion of college costs that should more properly be treated as an investment in the future would turn out to be higher than the 12 to 15 percent figure that is obtained when all of the cost is treated as an investment in future earnings.

If in this sense the obtained rate is an underestimate of the true one, it is also a misleading figure in another sense. The reason is that the whole exercise of calculating the rate of return seems to imply that the higher earnings of college graduates are attributable to what they learned in college. This implication is faulty. It has long been known—indeed it is taken for granted—that persons who graduate from college are on the average brighter than persons with less education. College graduates therefore have not only the advantage of more education but also the advantage of greater intellectual ability. How much of their higher earnings should be credited to each of these advantages? Some years ago Joseph Smith and I secured information about the then current earnings of groups of men who had graduated from high school some years earlier in Illinois, Minnesota, or Rochester, New York.[6] We also secured the high school records and intelligence test scores that each man made in high school and information about the socioeconomic status of his childhood home. At the time they graduated from high school, all of these men seemed qualified to go on to college. Some did; others did not. We compared the earnings of their mature years with their post-high-school education, with their ability as indicated by grades and intelligence test scores, and with the socioeconomic status of their parents. All three variables were positively related to

[6] Dael Wolfle and Joseph G. Smith, "The Occupational Value of Education for Superior High School Graduates," *Journal of Higher Education*, vol. 27, no. 4 (1956): 201-213.

earnings. The brighter ones earned more than the less bright. Those from favored homes earned more than the ones who had been reared in less favored homes. And the ones who had graduated from college earned more than the ones who had not. Of the three variables, education seemed to be the most important. We concluded that differences in ability and background accounted for perhaps a third of the difference in later earnings and that differences in education accounted for perhaps two thirds of the earnings differential.

A few other analyses have led to similar conclusions: a substantial part of the earning advantage of the college graduate is attributable to qualities he exhibited before he entered college, but a larger part of the graduate's advantage can be attributed to something that happened during his years in college. From the standpoint of later earnings, two related but not identical things happened during those college years: the graduates gained in knowledge and some of them acquired entrée to the higher paying professions that are not open to nongraduates.

Recently Paul Taubman and Terence Wales of the University of Pennsylvania have reanalyzed our data in a more penetrating fashion than we used earlier.[7] They found, as had we, that both education and ability were related to earnings and that education was the more closely associated variable. Some of their other findings were more surprising, however, and make it

[7] Paul Taubman and Terence J. Wales, "Effects of Education and Mental Ability on Income: The Evidence of the Wolfle-Smith Data," to be published as an Occasional Paper by the National Bureau of Economic Research.

80

desirable to present some cautions before those findings are discussed.

The Wolfle-Smith data came from a variety of large and small high schools in three states, but the data from Minnesota were more detailed and complete, and it is these data that Taubman and Wales could therefore analyze in detail. Minnesota is probably much more nearly representative of the United States as a whole than are many states, yet it is only one state, and what follows is based entirely on high school graduates from that one state. Moreover, the men involved all finished high school in the same year, 1938. In 1953, when we collected information about their occupations, earnings, and post-high-school education, they had all been out of high school for fifteen years, but because of World War II and because of different amounts of time in college or university, they had been working in their different occupations for quite different amounts of time. Some had probably already risen about as far as they would go, while others could surely look forward to substantially higher earnings later on.

In considering the following comparisons, it must therefore be remembered that all of the men were Minnesota high school graduates, the careers of many had been interrupted by World War II, and the earnings records were for the year 1953 for men then in their early thirties. Salary levels would all be higher now, and some of the differences might be larger or smaller. Nevertheless, these are the best data available (it is high time for a more comprehensive, detailed, and up-to-date study), and major relationships of the kind involved

81

usually change rather slowly. For these reasons, the results are worth considering, despite the cautions. To avoid any confusion between 1953 and current income levels, all of the comparisons are given in percentage terms.

Let the basis of comparison be the high school graduate whose intelligence score fell in the bottom 40 percent of all high school graduates and who did not go on for any formal education beyond high school. His 1953 income is arbitrarily given a value of 100. The earnings of other men can then be compared with this base. Men whose intelligence scores were in the range from the 40th to the 90th percentile earned, on the average, about 110. Men whose intelligence test scores were in the top 10 percent of all high school graduates earned about 130. Men who went to college for less than two years had an average annual income of about 120. Men who went to college for two or more years but did not graduate earned incomes of about 140. Men who graduated from college earned, on the average, about 150 if their intelligence test scores were in the lower 90 percent of all high school graduates, but those whose intelligence test scores were in the top 10 percent of all high school graduates had incomes that averaged about 200. Men who earned both a bachelor's degree and at least one higher degree had average incomes of about 160 if their intelligence test scores were in the lower 90 percent of all high school graduates, but those whose intelligence test scores were in the top 10 percent of all high school graduates averaged about 220 in income.

At the level of the top 10 percent on the intelligence

scale, there was significant interaction between intelligence and education. The income advantage was twice as great for men of this intelligence level who had received bachelor's or higher degrees as for men of lesser intelligence but the same amount of education. From the standpoint of their own later earnings and from the standpoint of society, if we assume that men are paid what they are worth to society, it is particularly important to get the top 10 percent through college or through graduate or professional school. The added income (and contribution?) of one such man equals the added income of two graduates of lesser ability.

To understand the differences in average income, it is necessary to consider another variable in addition to ability and post-high-school education, namely, the field of work entered. Earnings are higher in some fields than in others, and although each field includes men of varying ability and education, the higher paying fields tend to attract men of greater ability and higher education. The three broad occupational areas that offer the highest earnings are: the professions, including law, medicine, dentistry, engineering, the natural and social sciences, etc.; the semiprofessional fields, including managers and owners of various businesses and other kinds of establishments; sales positions, including insurance, real estate, and stock salesmen, as well as wholesale and retail salesmen. These three occupational categories included nearly all of the college graduates and about two thirds of the men with some lesser amount of post-high-school education. They also included practically all of the brightest men, regardless of the amount of education beyond high school. On the other hand, the men who did not go beyond high school were mostly employed in clerical, skilled, semiskilled, and service occupations, fields in which wages are not as high as in the professional, semiprofessional, and sales occupations.

Among all of the men engaged in professional, semi-professional, and sales occupations, those with higher intelligence-test scores earned more, but the amount of post-high-school education was unrelated to earnings. Bright salesmen earned more than less bright salesmen, but college graduate salesmen did not earn more than high school graduate salesmen of the same intelligence level. Among the men employed in clerical, service, and other less well-paying jobs, neither education nor intelligence was significantly related to earnings. In general, among the men who got into a particular kind of work, differences in education were not reflected in income, and differences in ability were related to income only in the more specialized and professional fields.

Not all of these findings are in agreement with other data, for example, with the Bureau of the Census report that more highly educated craftsmen and foremen earn more than do less well-educated men in the same fields.[8] The findings are subject to the cautions expressed earlier and will in any event be subject to revision whenever a more comprehensive study is carried out. Nevertheless, the Taubman-Wales analysis must be taken seriously. Its conclusions will surely be disturbing to ardent advocates of the benefits of education in the liberal arts,

[8] U.S. Bureau of the Census, *Present Value of Estimated Lifetime Earnings*, Technical Paper No. 16, Washington, D.C., U.S. Government Printing Office, 1967.

the sciences, a school of business, or some other preferred curriculum. Too often our beliefs in the virtues of
one or another kind of education have depended on
faith, hope, or charity, rather than on hard fact. Perhaps
the Taubman-Wales conclusions will challenge their
critics to investigate more thoroughly the outcomes of
college education. They may find solid evidence that
education, independent of ability and independent of
the field of work entered, makes a positive contribution
to a man's earning ability, and they may find better evidence than we now possess of other kinds of benefits.

As for now, however, Taubman and Wales conclude
that the principal economic benefit of a college degree
is that it provides admission to fields that would otherwise be difficult or impossible to enter. Admission to
some of these professions depends upon a sufficient
mastery of an organized body of knowledge and technique to be able to practice medicine, teach economics,
conduct research in chemistry, or do whatever else the
particular profession or specialized field requires. Higher earnings in these professions can therefore be considered as an earned return on the cost of acquiring the
requisite knowledge and skill. Formal education is not
the only way, but is probably the most satisfactory and
economical means, of acquiring those prerequisites.
Whether, in these cases, we wish to base licensing requirements on formal educational attainment depends
on other factors. There is little objection to the requirement that no one can practice medicine without
an approved medical education, even though a person
could acquire substantial medical knowledge without
going through the usual educational program. Nor is

there serious objection to the fact that a license is not required to teach in a college or university, even though the university professor who has earned no degrees is a rarity.

There are other professional fields in which college graduates are preferred, even though college graduation is not essential. Engineering is usually thought of as a professional field for graduates of schools of engineering, but about 40 percent of engineers are not college graduates. Many positions in business and management are open both to graduates and nongraduates. In these fields and in others that do not have formal or legal entrance requirements, employers still have the problem of selecting the most promising applicants. One easy method of screening out a large number of unlikely candidates is to require a college diploma. In this case, education serves as a screening device, not as an essential preparation.

The practice of using college graduation as a means of screening applicants shifts to society as a whole and to college graduates themselves part of the selection costs that would otherwise have to be borne by the employer. In some cases this may be the most economical means of solving the selection problem, but to some extent the practice is surely undesirable. Whenever employers place more emphasis on the possession of a degree than is warranted by the requirements of the work to be done, they lessen the opportunities for able young people who do not want or cannot afford to go to college, and they increase the pressure on young people to remain in school after they would rather be working and after many of them might better be working. Overemphasis on degrees and diplomas has created a credentials barrier that simplifies an employer's selection problems but that discriminates against young people who have the necessary abilities but not the required formal credentials.

The general conclusion from this analysis is that the 12 to 15 percent rate of return on the cost of going to college is explained in the following terms. Part of the earning advantage results from the graduate's ability to enter the relatively high-paying professions for which higher education is either a justified requirement or an effective screening device. Part of the earning advantage results from the fact that graduates are generally brighter than nongraduates. Part of the earning advantage is associated with the head start given college graduates by homes that, on the average, ranked higher in socioeconomic terms than the homes of nongraduates. The residual, and probably a relatively small residual, part of the earning advantage may be attributable to the knowledge and wisdom acquired in college other than that required for admission to some of the professions.

As for the graduates who become salesmen—and those who follow any other field of work they might have entered without a college degree—there are two things to be said. One is that even though some of them may earn no more than they would have earned without going to college, they still have had the consumption values of college attendance and they still have whatever cultural advantages they acquired. These are not without value. The other thing to say is that graduates who become salesmen should understand what they are doing. Much that has been said and written about

87

the value of higher education has clouded over the relationships that I have tried to make explicit in the last
few pages.

From the private individual viewpoint, the conclusion is abundantly clear: a college education is a good
investment. This conclusion holds whether the graduate's higher earnings are attributable to what he learned
in college or whether his diploma served as an admission ticket to one of the higher paying professions. The
conclusion holds with special force for students of high
intellectual ability. They can expect especially attractive financial bonuses for completing college or for continuing on through graduate or professional school. If
family finances or the scholarships which many of them
can secure are not sufficient to pay all of the costs, they
can well afford to borrow the rest.

Social Investment in Education

Students pay part of the costs of their education, and
they give up the money they might have earned during
college years, but they do not pay all of their educational costs. For the year 1966-67, the Office of Education
reported that society paid, in taxes, endowment earnings, gifts, and so forth, 80 percent of the direct educational costs of students in public colleges and universities and 56 percent of the costs of students in private
colleges and universities.

If it is reasonable to calculate the private rate of return on that portion of the cost (including foregone earnings) that is paid by the student, it is equally reasonable
to calculate the social return on the portion of the cost
that is borne by society. In order to make such calcula-

tions, it is necessary to have some measure of the return to society. An acceptable first approximation of the social return can be made by assuming that each man is paid what he is worth and that his earnings therefore constitute a fair measure of his worth to society. Although anyone could name acquaintances whom he considers to be paid more or less than their true worth, treating earnings differentials as if they equaled social value differentials is a reasonable basis for making the necessary calculations. Working in this way, Gary Becker has estimated that the rate of return to society on the money it invests in higher education may run to about twice the rate of return to the individual on his educational costs, or to a return rate of about 25 percent.[9] (In countries, in which society bears a larger fraction of the cost than is customary in the United States, e.g., Great Britain, the social return is likely to be correspondingly smaller.)

Only in a quite general way has society treated educational expenditures as an investment. If the responsible government agencies were to try to allocate funds for education in such a way as to produce the largest social gain, the allocation might be quite different from what it is at present. Figure 11 shows the private rate of return at the secondary school level to be much higher than at the college level. Perhaps that is also true of the social return. In Great Britain, on the basis of somewhat limited data, Mark Blaug came to the tentative conclusion that there was no underinvestment in higher education but that there was evidence of underinvestment in some forms of secondary education, particu-

[9] See note 5 above.

larly in the training of technicians.[10] There is similar evidence from some other countries.

One could make a good argument (at least until better data become available) that the greatest rate of return in the United States might result from heavier investment in the improvement of elementary and preschool education. Psychologists and sociologists have been giving a good deal of attention to the relations between early environment and intellectual development, or to the effects of the first few years of an infant's life on the course of his later development. Whatever one thinks about the relative importance of genetic and environmental factors, and the interaction between them, in accounting for individual differences, after a child is born it is only the environment that can be improved. There is still a good deal of uncertainty over how best to go about this task, but many of the people who have been working on problems of early childhood education are convinced that improved methods of child training and education would bring substantial and lifelong benefits. It may be that one of the most efficient ways of increasing the number of qualified college students would be to devote a larger part of our educational efforts, and budget, to providing a better start in life for children whose own homes are not conducive to good early development.

Even the most ardent advocate of such a view would not, however, want to make higher education entirely a private responsibility. We will continue to spend

[10] Mark Blaug, "The Private and the Social Returns on Investment in Education: Some Results for Great Britain," *The Journal of Human Resources*, vol. II, no. 3 (1967): 330-46.

large amounts of public money on colleges and universities, and it therefore remains appropriate to try to analyze how that money can be most effectively used. Although the marginal productivity model has in the past generally been used in calculating the social returns on educational investments, it is probably not the best model. The people who spend a year or two in the Peace Corps or in the VISTA program often feel well rewarded for their work, but little of that reward is in money. University and college professors as a group are widely considered—particularly among academicians—to be paid less than their true worth to society. In many fields, the range of salaries is not as great as the range of accomplishment. The greatest scientists and scholars receive honors that distinguish them from their more ordinary fellows, but their salaries are little, if any, higher. The best book may receive a Pulitzer Prize, but it is the most popular book, not the best one, that earns huge royalties. In short, there are many exceptions to the assumption that money income measures social worth.

George Psacharopoulos has recently tried to get around this difficulty by analyzing educational costs and returns in terms of social products instead of market earnings.[11] Such an analysis necessarily involves a number of assumptions, some of which might be challenged by other analysts, and the analysis dealt with Greece rather than with the United States. His results must therefore be taken as suggestive only. Nevertheless, it is interesting to find that between 1954 and 1965 in

[11] George Psacharopoulos, "Estimating Shadow Rates of Return to Investment in Education," *The Journal of Human Resources*, vol. V, no. 1 (1970): 34-50.

Greece, the return on the cost of promoting a secondary school graduate into a university graduate fell from a relatively high positive level to a negative level. In other words, Greece had so many university graduates in 1965 that what each added to society was not worth what it had cost to give him his university education. In contrast, the return on the added cost of bringing semiskilled and skilled workers up to the technician level (roughly the difference between primary and secondary education) increased markedly between 1954 and 1965. The general implication of these findings—as pointed out earlier—is that the return on educational costs cannot be considered alone. It depends upon the economy in which a graduate must work and upon the society he will serve.

So far in this discussion, higher education has been treated as if colleges and universities were all identical. Everyone knows they are not, and it is widely believed that different institutions have quite different effects on their students. College differences and their effects on students have been studied by Alexander Astin and his colleagues at the National Merit Scholarship Corporation and later at the American Council on Education.[12] Two kinds of effects can be distinguished by asking two questions. How do different kinds of colleges influence their students in terms of dropout rates, the

[12] Alexander W. Astin and Robert J. Panos, *The Educational and Vocational Development of College Students*, Washington, D.C., American Council on Education, 1969. See also, Alexander W. Astin, "Undergraduate Institutions and the Production of Scientists," *Science*, 141 (1963): 334-38; and Alexander W. Astin, "Undergraduate Achievement and Institutional 'Excellence,'" *Science*, 161 (1968): 661-68, as examples of some of the individual studies summarized in the volume by Astin and Panos.

choice of major fields, the tendency to go on to graduate or professional schools, and occupational plans? How much influence do quality differences among colleges have on what their students learn?

As groups, the students who graduate from different colleges are quite different. In terms of knowledge, future plans, occupational aspirations, and in a variety of other ways, the graduates of one college may have little resemblance to the graduates of a very different college, but the same can be said of their freshmen. Astin was not trying to compare the graduates of one college with the graduates of another. His problem was to find out what difference it made to a particular kind of student whether he went to one or another kind of college. He has been able to answer this question because he has obtained much information on many thousands of students who enrolled in several hundred quite different colleges and universities.

On this basis, the answer to the first question stated above is that different colleges do have different effects. The college a particular student chooses to attend influences his choice of major subject, his occupational plans, his decision whether or not to go on to graduate or professional school, and whether he stays long enough to earn a degree or becomes a dropout.

The answer to the second question is that a student's achievement as measured by the scores he makes on subject matter tests (specifically, the three area tests of the Graduate Record Examination) is almost completely independent of the quality level of the college he attends, the average intellectual level of his classmates, the financial resources of the institution, and the level

93

of academic competitiveness of the student body. His achievement test scores are, however, closely related to the aptitude test scores he made at the time of college entry. The bright, able freshman is likely to earn good marks on the Graduate Record Examination when he becomes a senior, whether his four college years were spent at Princeton or at Podunk. And the mediocre freshman is likely as a senior to make mediocre scores on the Graduate Record Examination whether his college years were spent at a "good" college or a "poor" one.

From the standpoint of assessing the intellectual effects of a college education, or from the standpoint of widely held ideas of academic quality, the second answer is the more disturbing one. From the standpoint of the student's later career, the first answer is more important. A particular student, with his particular pattern of abilities and interests, is more likely to become a college graduate if he enrolls in a privately controlled institution of higher education than if he enrolls in a public one. If he attends a liberal arts college, he is more likely than if he attends a university to continue on to graduate school, and more likely to become a scientist, a physician, or a teacher. On the other hand, if he enrolls in a large university, he is more likely to end up in law or business.

Moreover, the college he chooses helps to determine whether his classmates will be from one part of the country or another, whether they come from relatively affluent or less affluent homes, whether in large numbers they will go on to graduate or professional school. To a substantial extent these differences will persist in characterizing his friends and colleagues in later life.

94

The prestige of the undergraduate college he attends helps to determine his chances of getting into a prestigious graduate school or professional school. In fact, the circles in which he will move as a graduate student, as a medical student and physician, as a lawyer, a scientist, or a businessman are to a considerable extent determined by his undergraduate college.

In short, even though what he learns, as measured by scores on the Graduate Record Examination, may depend almost wholly upon personal characteristics that were well developed before he entered college, and may be only slightly influenced by the particular college he attended, the choice of college is nevertheless important in determining what he will become, the field of work he will enter, and his lifetime income. If "success" is his goal, he is right in striving to get into the "right" college.

An important link between studies of the private economic value of higher education and the differential effects of different kinds of colleges and universities has recently been provided by Andre Daniere and Jerry Mechling.[13] They have related the future earnings of college students, over and above what they could have expected to earn had they not gone to college, to the students' levels of intelligence and to the different quality levels of the colleges and universities they attended.

Male students were divided into five quality levels according to the 1965 national distribution of male high school graduates on the Scholastic Aptitude Test:

[13] Andre Daniere and Jerry Mechling, "Direct Marginal Productivity of College Education in Relation to College Aptitude of Students and Production Costs of Institutions," *The Journal of Human Resources*, vol. V, no. 1 (1970): 51-70.

(1) the top 1.5 percent; (2) the next 8.5 percent; (3) the next 20.0 percent; (4) the next 45.0 percent; (5) the bottom 25.0 percent. Colleges and universities were grouped into three "quality" levels, using as an index of quality the average instruction costs per pupil for the year 1963-64: (A) over $1,900 a year; (B) $1,000 to $1,899 per year; (C) less than $1,000 per year. Essentially none of the top 1.5 percent of students attended colleges of the C level and none of the bottom 25 percent of students attended colleges of the A level. With these exceptions, students of all levels were to be found in colleges of each group.

The authors then calculated the discounted lifetime earnings of each level of student if he entered each type of college. These values are shown in Table 4. The

TABLE 4

Discounted Lifetime Earnings of
Male College Entrants, by College
Aptitude and Institutional Quality

Instruction Cost Level	Aptitude Level				
	1	*2*	*3*	*4*	*5*
A	$200,105	$196,210	$177,865	$170,386	———
B	188,247	180,794	157,857	149,827	$145,059
C	———	168,711	150,341	137,999	128,945

SOURCE: Daniere and Mechling, "Direct Marginal Productivity of College Education."

figures there are not the actual lifetime earnings, but rather the discounted value of those earnings, at 6 percent, at age 18. The averages in the table include students who graduate and those who leave before graduation. In general, students of greater ability can expect higher earnings than students of lesser ability, and students who go to colleges of higher quality can expect greater earnings than those who go to colleges of lesser quality, but the differences are not large, and there are cost factors to take into account.

From the amounts shown in Table 4, the authors subtracted the discounted value of the earnings each group of students might expect if they did not go to any college, and then divided the remainders by the dis-

TABLE 5

Ratios of Discounted Differential Earnings
to Discounted Cost of College Education for
Male College Entrants, by College
Aptitude and Institutional Quality

Instruction Cost Level	Aptitude Level				
	1	2	3	4	5
A	5.36	5.50	4.85	4.64	—
B	7.69	7.43	5.61	5.17	4.80
C	—	12.44	10.06	7.79	5.62

SOURCE: Daniere and Mechling, "Direct Marginal Productivity of College Education."

counted cost of those attending college. The resulting ratios are shown in Table 5. The figures in this table are not rates of return, of the type discussed earlier, but are ratios. For example, the figure 5.50 means that if a second level male high school graduate attends an A level college, he can expect to increase his lifetime earnings over what he could expect if he did not go to any college by 5.50 times his college costs. (The ratio is actually between discounted values,

97

at age 18, at 6 percent.) Note, however, that if he enrolls in a C level college, the ratio is more than twice as great.

Several implications can be drawn from the two tables. The figures in Table 4 agree with those presented earlier in showing that men of higher ability can expect to earn more than those of lesser ability. At each ability level, the students who go to superior colleges can look forward to higher earnings than those who go to colleges of lower quality. This difference is greater for students lower on the ability scale than for those at the top. Top-quality students can expect an earnings bonus from attending a top-quality college, but the bonus is relatively greater for a mediocre student who can get admitted to a college of high quality.

If one considers the ratio of added earnings to college costs, instead of the earnings alone, colleges and universities of lesser cost—and presumably lower quality—appear to offer better bargains than do the expensive institutions. Daniere and Mechling conclude that these figures support the current policy of expanding higher education chiefly in the medium- and low-cost institutions, rather than in those of highest cost.

Conclusions

The findings and implications of the studies reported in this chapter lead to several conclusions. From the private or personal standpoint of an individual student, the costs of going to college are a good investment. The additional earnings he can expect throughout his lifetime may result primarily from the fact that possession of a degree will make it possible, or easier, to enter one of the better paying professions or fields of work, but whatever the explanation, he stands to benefit. This conclusion is especially strong for students near the top end of the ability scale. They are the ones who profit most from earning baccalaureate, graduate, or professional degrees.

Measured by what a particular student will learn in college, it does not make much difference which college he attends. In other respects, including later earnings, colleges and universities do have differential effects, and it is advantageous for a student to attend the best college or university that will accept him. If, however, he cannot be admitted to, or cannot afford to attend, an institution of comparatively high quality, he will be money ahead later on if he enrolls in a less expensive institution.

From the standpoint of society, it is advantageous to pay especial attention to getting the ablest high school graduates through college and in many cases through graduate or professional schools. They are the ones who will receive the highest financial return, and they are generally the ones who will make the greatest contributions to society.

How much society benefits from providing higher education for students of lesser ability is not so clear. Most of the analyses indicate that money spent on higher education is a good investment for society, just as it is for the individual. However, to the extent that employers raise their screening levels as the educational attainments of the population go up, it is quite possible that additional education may bring a private return to the individual without producing a commensurate social benefit.

The conclusion of Daniere and Mechling that public funds can be more efficiently spent by increasing opportunities in the moderate- and lower-cost institutions rather than in those of high cost must be considered in light of the fact that it is based solely on the rather narrow criterion of the ratio of added earnings to college costs. Universities have other functions than to increase the potential earnings of their students. Some of the consumption and cultural values may be just as great in institutions of lesser cost as they are in the more expensive institutions. Universities not only have to transmit knowledge to large numbers of students, they also have the responsibilities of adding to knowledge and of educating to the very highest levels the comparatively small number of students who will become the leaders and scholars of their fields. The fulfillment of these responsibilities is inherently expensive, and it is in the universities of highest quality that they are best conducted.

Finally, some of the implications of the studies reviewed call into question accepted educational values and beliefs. It is well to have accepted values challenged, but it is also necessary to keep in mind the fact that when attention is concentrated on the economic outcomes of higher education, some other elements of social policy may be forgotten. Ideas of equity, the belief that access to higher education should be determined by interest and ability regardless of personal financial circumstances, or faith in the intellectual

100

and cultural advantages of education in and of itself—such values as these must be involved in establishing or modifying educational policy, even though they have not been involved in the analyses summarized above. Those analyses concern only part of the proper basis for national policy. Moreover, their uncertainties indicate how desirable it would be to gain a better understanding of the economic, cultural, social, and intellectual values that are fostered by various kinds of institutions of higher education and by alternative policies for their support and further development.

4. Who Goes to College?

However one explains them, the advantages of higher education are substantial, and large numbers of young people seek to gain them, but not all do. What are the differences? Who are the people who go to college and earn degrees? In the main, the answer is: those who want to, plus those whose parents insist.

Some high school graduates who would like to enter college are prevented from doing so by lack of money, and some are prevented by other reasons, but lack of interest is the principal reason for not going to college. The surest way to find out which high school seniors will enter college is to ask them, but simply asking the seniors their plans is not very satisfactory to psychologists or others who study how college students are selected, why they decide as they do, or what the factors are that push some young men and women toward college and others away.

For the nation as a whole, and in round numbers, two thirds of the boys and half of the girls who finish high school enter college. Because 80 percent of all girls and 75 percent of all boys now finish high school, these percentages can be translated into percentages of the eligible age group who enter college. Again in round numbers, half of the young men and 40 percent of the young women of college age enter college.[1] Figures

[1] John K. Folger, Helen S. Astin, and Alan E. Bayer, *Human Resources and Higher Education*, Staff Report of the Commission on Human Resources and Advanced Education, New York, Russell Sage Foundation, 1970. On p. 153 there are references to many studies of factors associated with college attendance.

such as these quickly become out of date. The percentage of young people who complete high school has been climbing about 1.5 percentage points a year. As the percentage of the age group finishing high school continues to climb, the percentage going on to college does also. The percentage of young people who enter college has been rising by about one percentage point a year. And the percentage graduating from college has been increasing approximately half a percentage point a year.

Men are more likely to go to college than are women. They have been ever since the first colleges were founded and they still are, although the sex difference is much smaller now than it used to be. Students who earn better grades in school or who make higher marks on tests of intelligence or academic aptitude are more likely to enter college than are students who make lower grades or scores. Students whose parents have had more education or who stand higher on the socioeconomic scale are more likely to go to college than are students whose parents rank lower on this scale. There have been many studies of all three of these factors—sex, ability, and socioeconomic status. The detailed figures vary from one time, or place, or population to another, but the general trend is always the same.

The most comprehensive recent study of these matters is Project TALENT. This study began about ten years ago with the collection of a large amount of data on a nationwide sample of high school students. The data included test scores, grades, socioeconomic indicators, and educational and career plans. Periodically,

103

members of the sample are sent questionnaires to find out what has happened to them since the study began, or since the last follow-up.[2]

More limited in geographic scope, but excellent in its completeness and its detail, is a study of all of the high school graduates in the state of Wisconsin in the year 1957. William Sewell of the University of Wisconsin and his colleagues have been analyzing follow-up data on these students in terms of a variety of socioeconomic, educational, and interest variables.[3]

Data from these two studies on the relationships of ability and socioeconomic status with the probability of entering college are presented in Tables 6 and 7. Agreement between the two sets of data as to the relationships of the variables is reasonably high. Up-to-date figures would, however, be larger than those shown in the tables. The overall percentages of high school graduates who enter college is now higher than the figures shown in either table.

Consider all the high school graduates, of each sex separately, to be divided into fifths in terms of their scores on a standardized measure of academic aptitude. Of students in the bottom fifth of the Project TALENT sample in terms of academic aptitude, about 14 percent of the boys and 11 percent of the girls entered college, and most of them dropped out before long. At the other

---

[2] John C. Flanagan and William W. Cooley, *Project Talent One-Year Follow-up Studies*, Pittsburgh, University of Pittsburgh, 1966. There have been other, and will be still more, reports on this massive study of the later careers of a large national sample of high school students. Several special analyses of Project TALENT data are reported by Folger, Astin, and Bayer. See note 1 above.

[3] William H. Sewell and Vimal P. Shah, "Socioeconomic Status, Intelligence, and the Attainment of Higher Education," *Sociology of Education*, vol. 40, no. 1 (1967): 1-23.

TABLE 6

Percentages of High School Graduates in
Project TALENT Study Who Entered College
Immediately Following High School Graduation

Sex and Academic Aptitude	Socioeconomic Status					
	Low 20%	Low Middle 20%	Middle 20%	High Middle 20%	High 20%	Total
MALE						
High 20%	69	73	81	86	91	85
High Middle 20%	44	51	59	69	83	63
Middle 20%	30	35	46	54	67	46
Low Middle 20%	14	23	30	35	57	27
Low 20%	10	13	15	25	40	14
Total	24	40	53	65	81	49
FEMALE						
High 20%	52	61	66	80	90	75
High Middle 20%	24	35	41	58	78	49
Middle 20%	12	18	25	40	63	30
Low Middle 20%	9	10	16	24	54	18
Low 20%	9	9	10	16	41	11
Total	15	24	32	51	75	35

SOURCE: Special tabulations of Project TALENT data for the Commission on Human Resources and Advanced Education (in Folger, Astin, and Bayer, *Human Resources and Higher Education*, table 10.2).

end of the scale, from among the top fifth, about 85 percent of the boys and 75 percent of the girls entered college. High school graduates who fell in between the bottom and the top fifths of their classmates in terms of ability were also in between in terms of the percentage who entered college. There is, in short, a reasonably strong association between a student's ability and the likelihood of his entering college: the higher the ability, the greater is the likelihood. When socioeconomic status instead of ability was correlated with college en-

105

TABLE 7

Percentages of 1957 Wisconsin High School Graduates
Who Entered College, Classified by Sex, Academic
Aptitude, and Socioeconomic Status

Sex and Academic Aptitude	Socioeconomic Status				
	Low 25%	Lower Middle 25%	Upper Middle 25%	High 25%	Total
MALE					
High 25%	52	59	72	91	74
Upper Middle 25%	28	43	51	73	51
Lower Middle 25%	17	27	34	61	34
Low 25%	6	12	18	39	15
Total	21	34	45	73	44
FEMALE					
High 25%	28	37	48	76	55
Upper Middle 25%	9	24	31	67	35
Lower Middle 25%	6	20	26	44	23
Low 25%	4	9	16	33	11
Total	9	21	31	63	31

SOURCE: Sewell and Shah, "Socioeconomic Status, Intelligence, and the Attainment of Higher Education."

trance, a strong association was also found: the higher the socioeconomic status of the home, the greater the likelihood of college entrance.

In fact, the two correlations often turn out to be very similar. In the Project TALENT study, for example, 85 percent of the boys in the top one fifth in ability entered college and 81 percent of those from the top one fifth in socioeconomic status went to college. Of boys in the middle one fifth of the two distributions, the percentages entering college were 46 and 53. And from the bottom fifth of the two distributions, the percentages were 14 and 24. For girls, the relationships of ability and socioeconomic status with college are also similar. Of those in the Project TALENT sample who ranked in the top fifth in ability, 75 percent entered college. Of those in the top fifth in socioeconomic status, 75 percent went to college. For those in the middle fifth of the two distributions, the percentages were 30 and 32. From the bottom fifth, the two percentages were 11 and 15.

The three factors of ability, sex, and socioeconomic status do not act alone. All are related to college entrance, but they are also interrelated. When one takes account of sex, ability, and socioeconomic status, the differences in the probability of entering college become very large. Of the female high school graduates in the Project TALENT study who were in the bottom fifth in both intelligence and socioeconomic status, only 9 percent entered college. At the other extreme, of the women who were in the top fifth in ability and also in the top fifth on the socioeconomic scale, 90 percent went to college. The comparable percentages for men were 10 and 91.

The differences in these probabilities are sharp and regular. Yet it is noteworthy that none of the probabilities reach either zero or unity. Some high school graduates who have made good academic records and who have grown up in favored homes choose not to enter college. Some students from far down the academic scale and far down the socioeconomic scale get to college despite their unpromising records.

The question of whether ability or socioeconomic status is the more influential variable is subject to several answers. For Wisconsin boys, Professor Sewell concluded that differences in ability were more closely associated with attendance or nonattendance than were socioeconomic differences. For girls, the relative importance was reversed; socioeconomic status was more influential in determining which ones got to college. The Commission on Human Resources and Advanced Education concluded that socioeconomic differences are from one half to three fourths as influential as academic aptitude.

Whether one or the other measure is the more influential in a particular population, the conclusion is always clear that both are important and that the joint contribution of ability and socioeconomic differences accounts for about half of the variance.

This leaves the other half of the variance to be explained by a variety of other variables. All other things being equal, the members of some religious groups are a little more likely to go to college than are the members of others. The type of neighborhood in which a high school student lives, characteristics of the high school he attends, the attitudes and plans of his classmates, personality differences, the region of the country in which he lives—these and other variables are to small extents independently correlated with the likelihood of college attendance.

If other factors are allowed to vary as they will, young people of most of the minority ethnic groups—Negro, Spanish American, Indian—are less likely to enter college than are young people of the Caucasian majority, but if ability scores and socioeconomic status are held constant, there is very little difference in college attendance rates that can be attributed to race per se.

There are, however, significant differences in the colleges that are attended, and this difference illustrates the fact that all of the figures quoted so far on the probability of attending college are for colleges as a group. What has been counted is whether a student enrolls in any college, of any quality, anywhere. When one examines the actual colleges that are attended by different kinds of students, large differences become apparent. Students who are toward the upper end of the ability scale tend to go to the better and more selective colleges, while those toward the lower end of the scale tend to go to junior colleges and unselective four-year colleges. Similarly, students who come from middle- and upper-class homes are likely to enroll in the better colleges, while students who are lower in the socioeconomic hierarchy are likely to attend unselective colleges and junior colleges.

There are exceptions to this trend. For example, 6 percent of the top-quality students enroll in junior colleges of low selectivity. The general trend, however, is so strong as to make large differences from one campus to another in terms both of ability and family background of the student bodies. Institutions of high and very high selectivity enroll one third of all students, but two thirds of those in the top 20 percent of their high school classes. The universities that grant Ph.D.'s enroll a third of all students, and half of the top group.

The other variables that are associated with college attendance—sex, race, religion, region of the country, and socioeconomic status—also help to determine the kind of institution a student is most likely to enter. There is almost zero overlap in the groups of applicants for admission to Princeton, Evergreen State College,

Sweet Briar, and Grambling. The stream of students that flows out of high school and into college can be divided into overlapping but nevertheless quite different streams that enter different kinds of colleges.

Half of all students who enter college earn bachelor's degrees. This is one of the few educational statistics that has remained stable over a long period of time. The ratio of one graduate to two entrants has persisted for some forty years. Moreover, the ratio is essentially the same for men and women. In the 1960-64 period, the proportion of men averaged 51 percent, just two points above the women's average of 49 percent.[4] The rates are very different, however, in different colleges. In general, the more selective the admissions policy, the higher the percentage of entrants who earn degrees. Ivy League colleges give degrees to most of their entrants, while the nonselective junior colleges enroll few students who ever earn degrees.

Essentially the same variables that are correlated with college entrance are also correlated with educational persistence and the earning of degrees. The strength of the relationship changes, however. At successively higher educational levels, the socioeconomic status of the home becomes less and less useful in indicating which students will go on to the next higher level.[5] The net result of the selection that goes on after students enter college is that while on the average college graduates are brighter than college entrants and graduate students are brighter than college graduates,

[4] See note 1 above.
[5] Sewell and Shah (see note 3 above) analyze this point in some detail.

110

there is a wide range of ability among the persons who hold any academic degree.

Most of the work on the factors related to college attendance has been purely descriptive. The results have been summarized as correlation coefficients or in tables showing associations among variables. This kind of information is useful, but it does not give as much understanding of the causal relationships as we would like to have. In order to understand better what is happening, we need to know why students choose as they do. Fortunately, some attention is now being given to methods of analysis that seek to determine the causal relationships. This is a promising development, but it has not yet progressed very far. In fact, it may never be possible to construct a model or a set of causal relationships that can give a complete explanation of students' educational and occupational choices, but it is possible to make a start in this direction, as some psychologists and sociologists have already set out to do. One of these pioneers is William Sewell, whose work on Wisconsin high school graduates has already been cited. The following suggestions are based upon his work.[6]

If we try to list the principal causal linkages that determine an individual's educational and occupational achievement, the list would surely include those shown in Figure 12. This figure attempts to portray in schematic fashion the major elements and relationships in the causal chain that starts with a child at birth, or before, and that ends with his occupational attainment

[6] William H. Sewell, Archibald O. Haller, and Alejandro Portes, "The Educational and Early Occupational Attainment Process," *American Sociological Review*, vol. 34, no. 1 (1969): 82-92.

Figure 12

Schematic Representation of the Relations Among the Many
Factors That Determine a Person's Educational and
Occupational Attainment

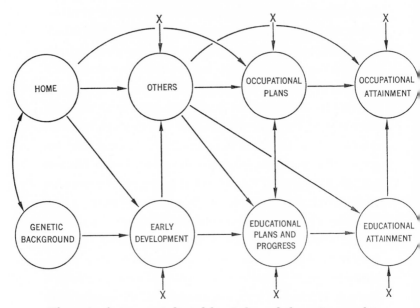

The major factors are indicated by circles and the major causal influences by arrows. The X's indicate other, sometimes unidentified,
influences.

as an adult. The major elements in the chain are indicated by circles and the major causal influences by
arrows, but not all of the important influences can be
indicated, and some may not even be known. Thus
there is an X with an arrow leading to each circle. The
X represents the other, perhaps unidentified, variables
that are influential. Approximately in chronological
order, but with a good bit of overlapping, the major
causal linkages in the chain are as follows.

1. A child's genetic background and physiological constitution, together with the way he is treated and trained by his parents and other persons in the home in which he is reared, determine the early development of his intellect and personality and his performance when he starts school. The "other factors" are not all known, but they include the characteristics of the school he attends, his teachers, his health, his playmates, and probably a number of other variables.

2. How a child develops during his early years and his performance after he starts school, plus the characteristics of his family and home, determine what influential persons expect of him. These influential persons may be his parents, his teachers, his classmates, or other persons who are important in his life. Sociologists sometimes call these persons "significant others." In expecting a youngster who starts out well in elementary school to continue to be a good scholar, these significant others are reacting to the child's own performance. In expecting the son of educated parents to enter college, they are reacting to the child's socioeconomic background. Again other factors are involved, and the significant others may expect the child to go to college because that expectation is congruent with their own background, values, or plans. There are probably still other factors involved that we have not identified.

3. The child's past school progress, plus the expectations of significant others, determine the child's future educational plans. If he does well in school, and if the people who influence him expect him to continue in school, he will probably do so. Other factors such as health, personality, and the attractiveness of alternative

113

courses of action also help determine how far he plans to continue in school.

4. The educational and occupational history, the aspirations, and the expectations of significant others determine his occupational plans. The additional factors involved at this stage include the opportunities he has had to observe adults in various occupational roles, the ideas he has formed of the duties, rewards, and disadvantages of various kinds of work, and a host of personality differences.

5. A student's educational and occupational plans influence each other. If he wants to become a lawyer or a doctor, he has to plan on an extended period of education. If he plans on college or on college and graduate school, he is likely to restrict his occupational choices to the kinds of work that require higher education or for which he thinks a college degree will be advantageous.

6. The student's educational plans, his occupational plans, and the expectations and advice of significant others determine the level of his educational attainment. The other factors here include the characteristics of the school or college in which he is enrolled, his own performance, and, of course, a variety of other influences, not all of which can be identified.

7. The student's educational attainment, his occupational plans, and the expectations and help of significant others determine his occupational attainment. The additional variables at this level include not only the influences that are effective during the educational and developmental period, but also the influences that affect his progress after he has entered his profession.

114

While such a scheme is the beginning of a causal model, it must be admitted that much of the influence is hidden in the category of "other variables" that must be included at each step. Using the method of path coefficients, Professor Sewell and two of his colleagues found the relative weight of "other variables," in the model on which I have based this one, always to be greater than the weight of the variables they could identify. This unsatisfactory state of affairs will probably continue for quite some time. Psychologists and sociologists are developing and testing theories of vocational choice; analyzing relationships among interests, ability, and attainment; and studying the personality variables that characterize persons in different occupational and professional groups. All of this work will be helpful, but there will be a great deal left unexplained in any model of the causal relationships that lead to educational and occupational attainment until we learn much more than we now know about human motivation. In order to understand why a person chooses the college, or the curriculum, or the occupation he does, we will have to know a great deal more about the general problem of why people do the things they do.

In any search for causal variables, much of the emphasis will probably have to be on patterns of family relationships and on childrearing practices. Family relationships and childrearing practices are correlated with parental education, socioeconomic status, and intelligence, but the correlations are far from perfect. Consequently, when we use information about socioeconomic status as an indication of a child's educational and occupational plans and aspirations, we are probably missing the variables that directly influence the child's behavior.

A quarter of a century ago, Alfred Baldwin and his co-workers found that changes over a three-year period in a child's I.Q. were not closely related to the level of his parents' intelligence, but were related to parental behavior. Casual, even indulgent, treatment was associated with the largest increases in I.Q.[7]

Several investigators have found large social class differences in the vocabulary used at home, the frequency of social interaction between a young child and older members of the household, and the encouragement and opportunities a child gets to explore, to make decisions for himself, or to experience new situations. Surely it is variables of this kind that are important here and not socioeconomic status per se. In comparing groups, socioeconomic status is a reasonably satisfactory predictor of school performance, but it is not a cause of high or low performance. To find the causes, we have to look deeper into the nature of a young person's experience.

The influence of significant others is undoubtedly related to socioeconomic level. At one extreme, a bright child from an upper-class home is probably subjected to the most consistent and homogeneous set of such influences. His parents expect him to go to college. His teachers, his classmates, his uncles and aunts, and his parents' friends all expect him to go to college. Some-

[7] Alfred L. Baldwin, Joan Kalhorn, and Fay Huffman Breese, "Patterns of Parent Behavior," *Psychological Monographs*, vol. 58, no. 3 (1945): 1-75.

times he rebels, but nine times out of ten he acts in accordance with these expectations. On the other hand, the bright child in a lower-class home encounters a greater variety of expectations and attitudes. A few of his friends plan to enter college, but most do not. His teachers may encourage him to plan on college, but his parents and relations and older friends may not.

This example of consistency or inconsistency in the influence of significant others is no doubt important in itself in helping to explain which young people enter college and which do not, but in a larger sense it is important as an illustration of how intricately intertwined are the many causal factors that are indicated in oversimplified fashion in Figure 12. If anyone is ever to understand fully how educational and occupational plans and achievements are determined, he will have to know a great deal more about motivation and behavior than anyone does now.

Changing Standards of Selection

It is of interest to inquire how the selection of college students has changed over the past decades. A much-debated question is this: As the percentage of young people who attend college has increased, what changes have there been in the average quality of college students? Informal answers to this question usually take one of two forms. One is the lament of older members of the faculty that college students are not as bright as they used to be. The other is the Old Grad's self-deprecatory admission that he is glad he got into college when he did, because his Alma Mater wouldn't accept him nowadays.

117

The Old Grad is right, and the old professor wrong. Many private colleges are more selective than they used to be, and many state universities have raised their admission requirements as junior colleges and state colleges opened their doors to applicants who could not meet rising university standards. As a result, in many individual colleges and universities, today's students are brighter than were yesterday's.

What is not so obvious—but nevertheless true—is that as higher education as a whole has expanded, the average ability level of entering freshmen, in all colleges and universities combined, has risen. This assertion violates the common assumption that when only a few students went to college, they were picked from among the brightest of our young people, and that as college enrollments have doubled and redoubled, the average quality must surely have gone down. College used to be for the intellectually select, the reasoning goes, and if we were getting the cream then, we must surely be dipping well below the cream line now. The common assumption is wrong. For forty or fifty years, up until the recent past and perhaps up to the present time, the average ability of college freshmen, as measured by well-standardized and comparable tests of academic aptitude, has been rising. Colleges have been getting more selective rather than less selective in admitting students.

Studies conducted in different ways, at different times, by different investigators, provide the evidence. In a nationally representative group of 167 colleges and universities, John Darley found the 1959 freshmen to

118

score a little higher than the 1952 freshmen.[8] The Commission on Human Resources and Advanced Education analyzed the 1961 and 1964 entrants in a sample of 280 institutions of higher education and found a significant rise in that three-year period.[9] A comparison of Project TALENT data for the early 1960's with my data for ten years earlier also showed a higher average level of academic aptitude for the later period.

Professors Taubman and Wales of the University of Pennsylvania have provided the most conclusive evidence in a recent reanalysis of all the sizable bodies of data they could find on the relationship between academic ability and college entrance.[10] They began with Robert Yerkes' classic report on the American soldier in World War I and continued on through studies by Viola Benson, Ralph Berdie, J. Kenneth Little, Wolfle and Smith, and others. In reanalyzing these studies, they determined, for each, the equation of the line showing the relation between ability and the probability of entering college. If such a line is perfectly flat, there is no selectivity at all; the high school graduate from the bottom of his class is just as likely to enter college as is the class valedictorian, but no one ever finds a flat line for this relationship. The line always slopes up, because the brighter high school graduates are always more likely than the less bright ones to go on to college. From

[8] John G. Darley, *Promise and Performance,* Berkeley, University of California Center for the Study of Higher Education, 1962.

[9] See note 1 above.

[10] Paul Taubman and Terence J. Wales, "Mental Ability and Higher Educational Attainment Since 1910," Discussion Paper No. 139 (multilithed), Philadelphia, Wharton School of Finance and Commerce, University of Pennsylvania, 1969.

the equations of such lines, Taubman and Wales derived indexes of selectivity. The higher the index, the greater the selectivity. These are the indexes they found for various past times: 1920's, .44; 1930's, .53; 1950's, .64; 1960's, .79.

Another way to show the trend is to plot the lines of relationship for two different time periods on the same axes. Figure 13 shows these equations for the 1920's and the 1950's. Students in the bottom third of their high school graduating classes were more likely to enter college in the 1920's than were students of the 1950's in the bottom third of their graduating classes. Above the 30th percentile, the difference was in the other direction. The abler students were more likely in the 1950's than in the 1920's to go on to college after they finished high school.

Still another way of showing the trend is given in Figure 14. The three curves of this figure have the following meaning. The upper one plots the average ability of high school graduates who entered college. There are irregularities in the curve, for the samples varied geographically and in their method of selection, but in general it has risen over the years. The middle curve plots the average ability of high school graduates who did not enter college. This curve has been falling slightly but fairly steadily. The bottom curve plots the difference between the average ability of high school graduates who went to college and high school graduates who did not. As time has gone on, there has been a gradual increase in the difference between average abilities of those who have gone to college and those who have not.

Figure 13
The Relation Between the Ability of High School Graduates
and the Probability of Their Entering College,
in the 1920's and 1950's

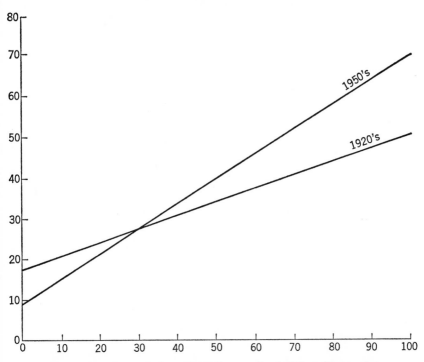

The steeper slope of this relationship in the 1950's indicates that
college entrants were more highly selected in terms of academic
ability in the 1950's than in the 1920's. SOURCE: Taubman and Wales,
Mental Ability and Higher Educational Attainment Since 1910.

It seems likely that in the short run, the trend toward
greater intellectual selectivity in the admission of college students will continue in the four-year colleges and
universities. In the junior colleges the story is different;
many of those colleges admit any high school graduate
who applies.

121

Figure 14
The Average Abilities of High School Students Who Did
and Those Who Did Not Enter College and the
Difference Between the Two, 1925-61

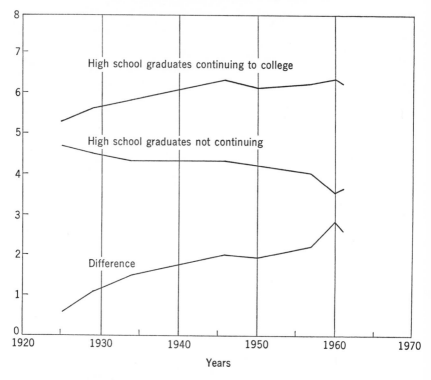

SOURCE: Taubman and Wales, *Mental Ability and Higher Educational
Attainment Since 1910.*

In the long run, a reversal of the trend must be expected. Almost all of the brightest high school graduates
are now entering college. If the percentage of high
school graduates who go on to college continues to
increase, most of the increase will, after a few more
years, have to be in students who are somewhat below
the top levels. When we reach that point, the average

122

quality will begin to decline. We are not yet there, however, and the broadening intellectual gap between the college population and the noncollege population presents a serious social problem.

This growing gap, plus the relative abundance of college graduates that can now be expected, seems likely to reinforce the tendency to require an undergraduate or an advanced degree for admission to a number of fields of work. Guild restrictions adopted by a number of professions take this form, and many employers insist that an applicant have a college degree. This requirement is justified if what is learned in the course of acquiring the degree is essential for effective practice, as most people would agree is the case in medicine, in teaching at the high school or college level, and in some other professions. In some fields of work, however, specific educational preparation at the college level is not essential. In these cases, a degree requirement is simply an easy way of screening out many unsatisfactory applicants. This is a gain for the employer, but the gain is achieved at the cost of disqualifying many men and women whose work would be satisfactory if they could only get started. An abundance of graduates and more selective policies of college admission will encourage the use of a degree as a job requirement, even though what was learned in college may not be essential for successful work.

As life gets more complex, ability and education do, however, become more necessary for success, especially for city dwellers. Increasing urbanization and the greater specialization and competition that are found in urban, as compared with smaller, communities will tend to prolong the competition for admission to selective

123

colleges, for in the city, social class, earnings, and job opportunities are more dependent on education than they are in a rural region. Consistent with this generalization is John Michael's finding that the correlations of both intelligence and socioeconomic status with college attendance is markedly higher in large and medium-sized cities than in smaller communities.[11] This finding, in turn, is consistent with the evidence presented earlier that the relation between intelligence and college attendance has been increasing during the several past decades of increasing urbanization.

The parental pressure on a child to qualify for admission to the "right" college is likely to continue, and perhaps to increase. With the increasing numbers of college graduates, with increasing urbanization, and with assortative mating resulting in strong tendencies for college-graduate men to marry college-graduate women, the pressure on their children to enter college will be great. These pressures will encourage—may even require—the more selective and better colleges to continue to be highly selective. Despite some current efforts toward egalitarianism in the admissions policies of some selective institutions, and despite the recommendation of Daniere and Mechling (see Chapter Three) that it would be good policy to place more second-level and average students in the better colleges, it appears likely that we must expect continued, and perhaps enhanced, intellectual stratification among colleges.

[11] John A. Michael, "On Neighborhood Context and College Plans (II)," *American Sociological Review*, vol. 31, no. 5 (1966): 702-706. Michael's paper comments on and reanalyzes some of the data originally published in William H. Sewell and J. Michael Armer, "Neighborhood Context and College Plans," *American Sociological Review*, vol. 31, no. 2 (1966): 159-68.

5. Mobility

Mobility is a characteristic of American society. A man moves from one coast to the other to accept a better position. Education helps the children of artisans and laborers climb social and economic ladders. The Peace Corps and urban improvement programs draw men and women from other jobs and other types of work. Our whole population shows substantial mobility, and most mobile of all are the members of the specialized professions. Movement from one region to another, from one type of work to another, from one employer to another, even from one specialty to another serves the wishes and ambitions of the individual as well as the needs of society.

When a man leaves one job to take another, he considers the relative advantages and disadvantages of the move as they affect him, his family, and his future prospects. He takes into account whatever personal, professional, social, or other aspects he values highly. The change is an important career decision which he makes on personal grounds. Sometimes he moves because a new job is positively attractive. Sometimes he moves because his old job has disappeared or because he is dissatisfied with it. Sometimes he moves because his company sends him to a new location or because the company that employs him merges with another company. Perhaps it is most generally useful to say that he compares the advantages and disadvantages of the alternatives open to him and chooses the one that on balance seems the most attractive.

In a nationwide study of why faculty members move

from one position to another, David G. Brown found that the typical professor put greatest weight on the work he would be doing and the quality of the colleagues with whom he would be working.[1] A faculty member considering a new position wants to know: What courses will I teach? What is the teaching load? What kind of students will I have? What research facilities and opportunities will be available? How competent are my prospective colleagues? The answers to these questions, Brown found, are more important to the typical professor than salary, fringe benefits, climate, academic rank, or other variables. Some faculty members are more idiosyncratic. They put highest priority on salary; they want to be near good skiing slopes; or they have other individualistic reasons for moving. Whether they follow the crowd or move for atypical reasons, the reasons are theirs, for each job change is an individual event, made for individual reasons.

High among these reasons is the opportunity to get a better job. By being mobile, men and women are able to take advantage of new and better opportunities. This, then, is the first advantage of mobility: the greater opportunity it provides individuals to move into the work they find most interesting or most rewarding. If men could not move from one job to another, each would be stuck for life in the kind of work or in the company he had chosen—or that had chosen him—at the beginning of his career. If the first job turns out to be the "right" job, there is no need to move. But often enough the first job, and sometimes the second and third ones also, are

[1] David G. Brown, *The Mobile Professors*, Washington, D.C., American Council on Education, 1967.

chiefly valuable in helping a young man to define the kind of position he will find most satisfying for the major part of his professional career.

Here is a situation in which what is good for the individual is also good for society. Society is benefited when workers are interested in their work, and society is benefited by the freedom workers have to move to new areas, new positions, and new kinds of work. In fact, labor mobility is one of the most effective means we have of keeping the supply of talent in reasonable balance with the work society wants done. It is not society, however, that makes most of the decisions. They are made by individuals, acting independently, and usually motivated primarily by what they consider their own personal interests.

The employer also thinks individually. If he has a vacancy, he looks for the man who appears to be best able to fill it. Usually he does not particularly care whether the new man comes from next door or from far away, and sometimes it makes little difference whether he comes from the same type of job or from a somewhat different type. Previous experience is often a highly relevant variable, and so the employer is likely to prefer someone who has been doing similar work. If, however, men with experience in closely parallel positions are not available, the employer selects someone from farther afield.

There are, of course, other means than job mobility to keep supply and demand in balance. When labor is in short supply, people come out of the labor reserve, for they are attracted by the salaries offered when labor is in high demand, or by the kinds of work available when

127

new opportunities develop. During the recent years of crowded school enrollment, thousands of married women who had earlier been school teachers and whose children had grown old enough to be in school went back to teaching. As another example, during the recent years of rapid increase in college enrollment, many retiring faculty members kept right on teaching, often at a different college or university. Sometimes the nature of a job is changed to allow persons of lesser training to perform part of it and to free scarce but fully trained professionals to spread their talents more widely. Immigration policies are sometimes changed to encourage persons with wanted skills to come from other countries.

However, of all of the means of adjusting the available supply of educated professionals to the work society has laid out for them, the most flexible, and the most interesting to analyze, is mobility. Census records of geographic movement regularly show members of the professional group to have moved more frequently and for greater distances than any other group of workers, even including salesmen. Where most workers move within a relatively local labor market, the market for professional talent is often national in scope, and in some fields international. During the recent decades of growing demand for professional talent, willingness to move, often over great distances and to quite different kinds of jobs, has enabled many thousands of professional men and women to advance themselves and to devote their talents to work of high priority.

From the standpoint of labor market adjustment, it is not necessary that all members of a discipline be equally mobile. If there is a shortage in one field and extra

128

people in another, movement of a comparatively small minority from the surplus to the shortage area will bring things back into balance. If there is an excess of engineers in Cleveland and a shortage in Denver, only a comparatively few Cleveland engineers need go to Denver to bring both cities into balance.

Although normally only a comparatively small number need move to restore balance, when professional opportunities change and expand as rapidly as they have in the past thirty years, the amount of movement may be substantial. In an average recent year, one professional man in ten has made a geographic move and one in twenty has changed from one kind of occupation to another.

From the standpoint of analyzing the labor market, it is useful to think of several kinds of mobility. The several kinds may be classified as mobility from one place to another, from one function to another (for example, from teaching to business management), from one type of employer to another (for example, from a labor union to the Office of Economic Opportunity), or from one specialty to another (for example, from chemistry to physics). All of these types of mobility are interrelated. And they are all related to education and ability. Moreover, they are substantially interchangeable in their effect on the labor market.

We usually think of a person as moving from one job to another, but Harrison White has discussed mobility in terms of a vacancy moving from one location to another.[2] This is an illuminating way to think of mo-

[2] Harrison R. White, *Opportunity Chains*, Cambridge, Harvard University Press, 1970.

bility. When a vacancy occurs, the employer looks for someone to fill that vacancy. When he succeeds, another vacancy is created. Then another employer looks for someone to fill his vacancy. When he succeeds, a third vacancy is created. And so it goes, through a longer or shorter chain, until the last vacancy is allowed to stay empty or until someone moves into it from outside the current labor force. Each vacancy in the chain can be filled by moving a man from some other part of the country (geographic mobility), from some other kind of work (functional mobility), from a different kind of employer (sector mobility), or from a different specialty (disciplinary mobility). Thus the several kinds of mobility are interchangeable in their ability to keep supply and demand in effective balance.

Follow-up studies of college graduates or Ph.D.'s and studies of professional groups, such as engineers, provide quantitative information on the amount of occupational mobility that has characterized the American scene in recent decades. In one class of Massachusetts Institute of Technology graduates, half had left their first jobs within three years, two thirds within four years, and three fourths within five years after graduation. In the fall of 1962, 11 percent of all college and university faculty members had taught at another campus the year before. By 1964 one fourth of all the Ph.D. recipients in science from 1957 through 1962 had moved from industry to teaching, from teaching to government service, or had made some similar shift.

In a rapidly growing field, mobility is especially high. Following the development of the transistor, solid state physics became a particularly active field of research

130

and development. Industrial demand expanded much more rapidly than did the number of university graduates who had specialized in solid state physics. The 1964 National Register of Scientists and Engineers included only 86 persons who held Ph.D. degrees in solid state physics, and only 46 of them were working as solid state physicists. The others had moved into other areas of physics, or into chemistry, engineering, and other fields. Many were no doubt still using their expert knowledge of solid state physics, for the transfer of knowledge and technique from one field to another is one of the reasons for and one of the advantages of transferring from one specialty to another.

Although there were only 86 Ph.D.'s in solid state physics in the 1964 Register, there were 1,894 Ph.D. holders who were working as solid state physicists. Of these 1,894 solid state physicists, 1,388 held Ph.D.'s in other branches of physics; 318 had earned that degree in chemistry; 109 in engineering; and 33 in a variety of other disciplines, including one who had earned the doctorate in horticulture but had since become a solid state physicist.[3] This is a striking example of the fact that a new field can expand rapidly by drawing into itself able people who have some of the necessary knowledge, skills, habits of thought, and methods of work, even though their formal training and previous experience lie in other fields. Migration across disciplinary boundaries is not as well understood or as often recognized as are geographic migration and other kinds

[3] National Academy of Sciences, *Doctorate Recipients from United States Universities, 1958-1966*, Publication No. 1489, Washington, D.C., National Academy of Sciences, 1967, p. 91.

131

of job changes, but it is one of the means of keeping supply and demand in reasonable balance.

At the individual level, there have been some notable examples of field changing. Jean Piaget is surely one of the world's best known psychologists. At age 15 he was publishing scientific articles on molluscs, and he earned his Ph.D. with a dissertation in malacology. It was only later that he became a psychologist. Hugo Eckener switched in the other direction. His fame was earned as a pioneer in the field of lighter-than-air craft and for his transatlantic and round-the-world trips with the Graf Zeppelin. Surely no one had expected this career change when Dr. Eckener was awarded the Ph.D. in psychology under Wilhelm Wundt.

The amount of movement from one field to another is greater than is often recognized. Table 8 shows the percentage of 1958 bachelor's and master's degree recipients in each of several fields who were still employed in their degree fields five years later. Some of the losses are easy to explain. Many of the women had married

TABLE 8

Percentages of 1958 Bachelor's and Master's Degree
Recipients Who, Five Years Later, Were Employed
in the Fields of Their Degrees

	MEN		WOMEN	
Major field of study	AB	MA	AB	MA
Business & commerce	59%	65%	21%	——
Education	76	88	91	83%
Engineering	77	75	17	——
Natural sciences	26	52	12	27
Social sciences	4	24	3	17

SOURCE: Sharp and Krasnegor, *Five Years after the College Degree.*

and left the labor force. In the natural and social sciences, bachelor's and often even master's degrees do not provide sufficient preparation for professional work. The percentage of women, and in some fields the percentage of men, who were not employed in the fields of their degrees is thus quite understandable. But graduates in business and commerce, education, and engineering are prepared for direct entry into the corresponding fields of work. In each of these areas a substantial number of the men—up to a third and more—had moved to another kind of work within five years of the time they earned their professional degrees.[4]

Table 9 shows the percentages of Ph.D. recipients in a number of fields who were still working in their degree fields two to seven years later. As would be expected,

TABLE 9

Percentages of 1957-62 Ph.D. Recipients Whose Employment in 1964 Was in the Same Field as Their Degrees

Field of specialization for Ph.D. degree	Percentage employed in same field 2-7 years later
Biochemistry	85
Biological Sciences	96
Chemistry	98
Earth Sciences	99
Economics	100
Mathematics and Statistics	100
Physics	99
Psychology	96
Sociology	100

Only native-born U.S. citizens are included in this table. SOURCE: Folger, Astin, and Bayer, *Human Resources and Higher Education.*

[4] Laure M. Sharp and Rebecca B. Krasnegor, *Five Years After the College Degree, Part II, Employment,* Washington, D.C., Bureau of Social Science Research, 1966.

field retention is higher at the Ph.D. than at the A.B.
or M.A. levels, but even at the Ph.D. level, substantial
numbers had left their degree fields. Table 10 gives
more detail on this point and shows that the number of
changes of specialization continues to increase with
time. In round numbers, for all fields combined, five

TABLE 10

Percentages of Ph.D.'s Whose Employment in 1962
Was in the Same Field as Their Degrees

Field of Doctoral Degree	Year of Doctoral Degree			
	1935-40	1945-50	1955-60	Total, All Years
Physiology	31%	49%	67%	52%
Pharmacology	23	40	77	52
Biochemistry	30	52	72	56
Microbiology	46	74	78	68
Botany	40	39	53	45
Genetics	31	41	60	47
Zoology	40	48	51	47
Other Biological Sciences	23	*	46	41
Medical Sciences	74	67	78	74
Agricultural Sciences	65	78	73	72
Psychology	71	82	90	81
Sociology	62	66	79	70
Economics	68	70	78	72
Political Science	68	75	81	76
History/Geography	68	75	85	77
Mathematics/Statistics	82	89	91	88
Physics	64	76	90	77
Chemistry	64	80	84	76
Geological Sciences	90	85	93	89
Engineering	80	87	92	87
Language/Literature	75	82	89	82
Arts/Humanities	53	70	82	69
Miscellaneous Professions	63	68	80	72
Education	66	76	81	76
Total	59	71	77	70

* Too few cases to compute percentage.

SOURCE: Harmon, *Profiles of Ph.D.'s in the Sciences*, pp. 113-16.

years after the doctorate 20 percent had moved out of their fields of doctoral specialization; fifteen years after the doctorate, 30 percent had changed; and twenty-five years after the doctorate, 40 percent had changed.[5]

There are substantial field-to-field differences in retention rates. Geologists and engineers are least likely to switch fields. Biologists appear to be most likely to change their fields of specialization, but caution is necessary in interpreting the figures, for there are more different specialty labels in biology than there are in the physical or social sciences. A change of interest is therefore more likely to result in a new specialty label for a biologist than for a chemist.

In all fields, however, changes of specialization, even among holders of the Ph.D., take place often enough to demolish the stereotype of the professional man who may change positions but who never leaves his chosen field. Understandably, the man or woman who has invested four or more years of graduate work in earning a Ph.D. is more strongly tied to his own specialty than is the person who left the university with a bachelor's or master's degree, but at all levels there is more field switching than we usually assume when we speak of students choosing their careers.

[5] Lindsey R. Harmon, *Profiles of Ph.D.'s in the Sciences*, Publication No. 1293, Washington, D.C., National Academy of Sciences–National Research Council, 1965. This report provides a large amount of information about the geographic, social, occupational, and field mobility of the men and women who earned Ph.D. degrees in the U.S. from 1935 to 1960. The Doctorate Record File of the Office of Scientific Personnel of the National Academy of Sciences–National Research Council contains a rich mine of information about the recipients of doctor's degrees from American universities from 1920 on. Much additional data on the mobility of doctoral degree holders will be included in a forthcoming report, *Mobility of Ph.D.'s.*

Job mobility is more important than are new entrants in filling vacancies and in keeping the supply of professionals adjusted to the changing work requirements. Brown found that 22 percent of all college and university posts in the fall of 1962 were filled by newly appointed men and women. Half of the new appointees had moved from another campus. A smaller number had switched to teaching from some other kind of work, such as industry or government. Still others were returning to teaching after a period of advanced study. Only the remaining minority of the 22 percent of new faculty members were new entrants to the professional labor force.[6]

This situation is generally true of the professions. In a well-established field that is not undergoing unusually rapid growth, most of the vacancies are filled by appointing someone who is already in the field and employed in a similar position elsewhere. When a field is undergoing very rapid growth, most of the vacancies are still filled by hiring people already in the professional labor force, but in this situation it is necessary to import some new talent from other kinds of jobs and other fields of work. The space program was built up rapidly in this fashion. The electronics industry had earlier been built up in the same way.

It is impossible to state quantitatively how much movement from one specialty to another occurs. Many of the professional labels are not tightly defined, and many of the professional boundaries are permeable. There is no ambiguity about moving from Cleveland to

[6] See note 1 above.

Denver. But when does a chemist cross the line that separates chemistry from biology?

Some apparent changes result largely from a difference in the prestige of different titles and may not indicate any major change in the kind of work being done. "Engineer" is a title of prestige. "Engineering technician" is not such a prestigious title. A year or two after completing their training, young men who graduate from technician training courses are likely to be classified as engineering aides, junior engineers, electronic specialists, maintenance managers, or to have other descriptive titles. With a little more experience, a good many of them will be called engineers.

The size of a field also helps to determine whether or not a change of work is accompanied by a change of label. Some chemists can change their work quite substantially and still remain chemists. When others change, they acquire new labels, for chemistry overlaps with biology, physics, and geology. Thus some biochemists easily become chemical biologists; other chemists become geochemists, and then geologists; and still others can move across a different boundary and become physicists.

In a study of mobility among Ph.D. scientists who were included in both the 1960 and 1964 National Register of Scientific and Technical Personnel, Milton Levine found some 2,300 who called themselves mathematicians in 1960.[7] Four years later, only about 2,000 of

[7] Milton Levine, "National Register of Scientific and Technical Personnel: A Data Source for Mobility Analysis," Paper presented at the Cornell Conference on Human Mobility, Ithaca, New York, Oct. 31-Nov. 2, 1968.

137

the original 2,300 still called themselves mathematicians. On the other hand, there were some 140 who classed themselves as meteorologists in 1960, but by 1964 another 70 scientists were calling themselves meteorologists. Because of the ambiguities of some of the professional labels involved, it is difficult to count the number of people who move from one specialty to another. Perhaps the most satisfactory method is to rely on what people call themselves. If a man with a Ph.D. in zoology stops calling himself a zoologist and says he has become a psychologist, for purposes of classifying the members of the labor force we should agree that he is a psychologist, for we have no better basis than his own testimony for deciding when a man has switched from one field to another. This was essentially the basis used in compiling the data for tables 8, 9, and 10.

Not much is known about the characteristics of people who switch fields and how they differ from their colleagues who remain in their original fields, but some speculation seems reasonable. Donald Glaser changed from physics to biology after winning the Nobel Prize in physics. Obviously failure in the original field is not always the reason for moving. In fact, it seems likely that there is positive qualitative selection. It takes boldness for a well-established physicist to decide to switch to a different field of science; he is unlikely to take such a gamble unless he sees important and challenging problems and has confidence in his ability to contribute to their solution. These are in themselves marks of intellectual vigor.

Yet in comparison with their colleagues who do not move, many of those who cross disciplinary lines are

138

probably not as visible to most members of the discipline. They are not the traditionalists whose interests lie close to the center of a discipline. Nor are they usually the people who have strong commitments to the discipline itself, the persons who write its basic texts or serve as its professional officers. They are more likely to be in one of the less specialized fields or subfields, to have interests that lie close to a disciplinary border, or to its applications, or to be interested in problems that are also of interest to persons in other disciplines. I suspect also that if we had the data, we would find that they are more varied in their interests and perhaps less traditional in their training than are the people from the middle of the field. In some senses they are certainly pioneers, free and willing to move into new fields and new kinds of responsibilities. Some of them moved into solid state physics. Earlier some of them—from physics, mathematics, engineering, and even from botany, economics, and psychology—developed the field of operations research. The space program attracted many of them. In general, those professionals who switch fields constitute a flexible and capable element of the labor force that makes it possible for new areas of work to develop rapidly.

No other country uses mobility as a means of labor force adjustment as extensively as does the United States. In France "the mobility of workers in private enterprise is more theoretical than real."[8] In the United Kingdom "it remains very difficult . . . for people to

8 Marcel Chapuy, "In-career Training of Highly Qualified Personnel in a Large Public Enterprise," in *Policy Conference on Highly Qualified Manpower*, Paris, Organisation for Economic Co-operation and Development, 1967, pp. 289-314.

139

make a change of occupation after the age of twenty-five. . . . It is still a matter of surprise (and for some even a matter for resentment) if a manager moves from (say) the chemical industry to the railways. . . . Such matters as prescribed arrangements for professional training and inflexible pension schemes combine with the natural inertia of organisations to limit opportunities for change of occupations."[9]

In Japan it is customary for industry and business to hire graduates directly from the schools and universities. "Thereafter, until age 55, when most of them are automatically retired, they receive automatic annual salary increases. From time to time, they are given status advancements with new titles, but usually their corporate caste is rigidly determined by the record they made in college and the ranking of the college they came from. A man from one of Japan's best schools enters corporate life with such a lead that it can't be overcome by a graduate from a lesser institution, no matter how talented."[10] Peter Drucker writes of this system: "The young educated Japanese . . . would be most unhappy were Japanese employers to abandon the tradition of 'lifetime employment.' They strongly resist all attempts to give the employer power to discharge any but top management people. But they increasingly demand for themselves the right to leave and go elsewhere, even though it is contrary to tradition. One Japanese company, Sony, the electronics manufacturer, has been highly successful in attracting unusually able people to

[9] C. F. Carter, "The Economic Use of Brains," *Advancement of Science*, vol. 18, no. 95 (1961).

[10] Scott R. Schmedel, *Wall Street Journal*, Nov. 18, 1969, p. 40.

its employ. This success is largely traced by Sony managers to their practice of offering senior jobs to able people who work for other companies and of helping employees who want to leave to find better jobs elsewhere—both in violation of Japanese custom. At the same time, every Sony employee has all the 'rights' of 'lifetime employment.' Once he has joined he can stay on the payroll until he retires if he so desires. The other Japanese employers are still afraid of such mobility. They fear that knowledge workers—engineers, accountants, or computer experts—will become migratory."[11]

The Japanese economy has been advancing at a rapid pace, while the British economy has been sluggish. Reasons for the difference lie elsewhere than in mobility rates, for in both countries it has been rare for professional workers to move from one employer to another. The amount of mobility is an important variable, but it is not the only one involved in productivity, nor is it the only means of labor market adjustment. In both England and Japan, a man's duties and responsibilities may be changed within the same company, and in Japan there has been a great deal of functional change within a company, for Japanese employers have put much emphasis on training and retraining workers to give them whatever skills become desirable. There are other methods of adapting the existing supply of workers to the changing needs of society, but the voluntary and flexible movement of workers to a new employer, a different region, or another function is probably the most rapid.

[11] Peter F. Drucker, *The Age of Discontinuity*, New York, Harper and Row, 1968, p. 253.

141

Claus Moser of the London School of Economics and Political Science has contrasted the United States with his own country in these terms:

> The difference between our respective situations can be characterized—in caricatured terms—in the following way. Toward one extreme, you have a rich country, in which a very high proportion of the children get to college, where they receive a broad, non-specialized education, as a result of which they have great occupational flexibility. . . . Thus, in the United States there is breadth and flexibility in job preparation. You therefore have high adaptability and substitutability in jobs. You also have a fairly fuzzy—to my mind, enviably fuzzy—job structure. You have great retraining programs, and, as a result, manpower shortages are rarely thought of as real bottlenecks. Instead, you rely on adjustments in manpower utilization in the short term, rather than on forecasting long-term shortages or surpluses.
>
> At the other extreme, also somewhat caricatured, are countries like England. We have a poor economic growth performance, with low densities of scientists and technologists and high level people generally and . . . a low proportion of the age group reaching higher education. We have an extremely specialized educational system which produces somewhat inflexible and unadaptable people, who in turn find themselves in a rigid job structure. Because of all this, we are bound to be worried about the matching of jobs and people and to want to forecast long-term needs. The more rigid your occupational and educational

worlds, the more you need manpower forecasting, and the more serious it is when they go wrong.[12]

Why mobility is so much higher in the United States than in other countries is partly a matter of the stage of development. Movement is more characteristic of a complex, technological, commercial society than of an agrarian one (it is no accident that the first large break in the Japanese tradition of occupational immobility was made by an electronics manufacturer), but that there are significant differences among the industrially advanced nations is illustrated by the experience of Japan, France, the United Kingdom, and the United States.

The American character and American history are no doubt involved. Everyone in the United States is either an immigrant or the descendant of a relatively recent immigrant. The West was settled by immigrants from the East and from foreign countries. A large geographic area with a common language and without national or customs barriers makes it much easier to move a thousand miles here than it is in Europe.

Geographic mobility may set the stage for other kinds of movement. Lloyd Warner and James Abegglen remarked that "the act of movement, spatially, establishes many of the preconditions for social and occupational mobility. The territorially mobile man is disengaged from the web of relations that determines his social position, and the son of an immigrant is that man least engaged with his cultural past. The physical mobility of Americans is a precondition to the changes in social

---

[12] Claus A. Moser, in "Symposium on Manpower Theory," *The Journal of Human Resources*, vol. II, no. 2 (1967): 218.

position that have been found to take place increasingly in American business."[13] America places great value on higher education, and more than half of American college students live away from home. Having made one geographic move, and having thus disengaged themselves—at least partially—from the web of relationships that characterized the position of their parents, they are likely to find it easier to make other moves later on.

The Encouragement of Mobility

American social history is not the only factor involved in the explanation of a high level of mobility. A number of practices and policies have been developed that encourage occupational mobility, and some have been deliberately developed for this purpose.

National scholarship and fellowship programs have been designed to attract students into fields in which a shortage existed or was expected. The graduate fellowships of the National Science Foundation were intended to increase the number of future scientists. The National Defense Education Act of 1958 offered graduate fellowships in fields in which shortages of college teachers were feared. Some scholarship and fellowship programs have been based solely on ability without regard to the student's field of specialization, but the custom is well established of using money to induce students to enter fields in which shortages are experienced or expected. Direct grants to students are not the only way in which the government can use money to attract people into an area. "Research and development funds act as an

[13] W. Lloyd Warner and James C. Abegglen, *Occupational Mobility in American Business and Industry*, Minneapolis, University of Minnesota Press, 1955, p. 27.

important magnet drawing highly trained scientific and technical manpower to the area or establishment in which the funds have been placed. The funds can also be a major factor in making actual scientists out of potential ones, for they frequently stimulate interest in education and the sciences in the affected areas."[14]

Some organizations require a person to be promoted within a certain period of time or to go elsewhere. Such an up-or-out rule has been adopted by many of the more prestigious universities and is followed by the military services. An assistant professor must either be good enough to be promoted to an associate professorship within, say, five years, or his appointment is terminated. The colonel who is not promoted to brigadier general within a given period of time is retired. Because both the assistant professor and the colonel are too young to retire from professional activity, they usually find other positions.

Industry has for some years been willing to pay the moving expenses of some of their new professional and executive staff members, and regularly pays the moving expenses of an employee who is reassigned to a different city. The Federal Government has more recently adopted similar practices. The Revenue Act of 1964 authorized payment of moving expenses specifically to promote labor mobility.

For many years the United States assigned immigration quotas to other countries in proportion to the number of previous immigrants from those countries. In

[14] U. S. Senate, Committee on Labor and Public Welfare, *The Impact of Federal Research and Development Policies upon Scientific and Technical Manpower*, Washington, D.C., U.S. Government Printing Office, 1966, p. 3.

1968 the basic policy was changed. National-origin quotas were abandoned and new quotas were set, partly to favor immigrants closely related to persons already living in the Uniterd States and partly to favor immigrants with skills or professional qualifications desired in the United States. Basing immigration quotas on professional or skill qualifications is a practice increasing in other countries as well.

The Teachers Insurance and Annuity Association pioneered a scheme for providing pensions for faculty members that would free them to move easily from one college or university to another. Under the portable pension plan of TIAA, and its more recent affiliate, the College Retirement Equities Fund, both employee and employer contribute to building up a pension fund that belongs to the individual. When he moves to a new campus, he takes his accrued pension rights along with him. Thus academic mobility is made easier than it was when many colleges and universities had pension plans that had to be forefeited by a faculty member who moved to another campus before retirement.

When the social security program was established in the United States, this idea of portability or full vesting in the individual was taken over bodily and became a part of our largest, national program for providing retirement income. The idea may become more widely adopted. In 1965 the President's Committee on Corporate Pension Funds recommended that the principle of full vesting be incorporated in all private industrial pension plans, and in 1968 the American Chemical Society began to investigate the possibility of a national scheme of fully vested pensions for chemists (and perhaps for other scientists) regardless of where they worked or of how often they changed jobs.

Early retirement encourages mobility. Many professional people who are active and vigorous at an early retirement age want to find another position. A few universities have taken good advantage of the early retirement policies of other universities. The University of Arizona is a notable example. While retiring its own faculty members at a reasonable age, it has added to its staff several nationally known scholars who have reached retirement age elsewhere; at the University of Arizona they have continued right on with productive careers of teaching and research, sometimes bringing their graduate students along with them.

The project grant system of the National Science Foundation, the National Institutes of Health, and other federal agencies has contributed to academic mobility, though not intentionally so. The scientist who could get government grants for his work became a particularly attractive appointee. If he moved, the granting agency was usually willing to transfer his grant to the new institution. And thus another practice conducive to a high level of mobility came into existence.

Sabbatical leaves, leaves of absence for professional advancement, and the arrangements that some leading industrial and business firms provide for mid-career periods of advanced study for promising members of the firm who are expected to rise to high levels of responsibility are usually granted with the stipulation that the person will return to his prior employment for at least a given period of time. Nevertheless, the fact of being away from the accustomed duties and environment and the experience of getting acquainted with new colleagues, new problems, and new surroundings increases the probability of a permanent move. Universities, industry, and government all recognize the advantages of giving promising men mid-career opportunities for advanced study, but they also know that some of the people to whom they grant leaves will not return, or will return only long enough to fulfill their obligations and will then be off to new posts.

Job requirements themselves sometimes require mobility. Some school systems will not employ inexperienced teachers. Other job requirements often specify a minimum period of prior experience.

The National Aeronautics and Space Administration did not invent, but did use effectively, the device of coining new position titles to facilitate occupational mobility. NASA needed a great variety of engineering, scientific, and managerial talent, and if its schedule was to be met, it needed to expand rapidly. There simply were not enough persons available who bore such appropriate titles as aerodynamicist, or aeronautical engineer. To make recruitment easier, and with cooperation from the Civil Service System, NASA developed new examinations and invented new titles, titles that differed from the labels under which university degrees were conferred, but that indicated the functional area involved. Titles that reflected functions and responsibilities made it easier to recruit and appoint people from diverse but relevant backgrounds. For example, a physicist who would have denied being an aeronautical engineer could be interested in appointment as an aerospace technologist.

148

Finally, mobility abets mobility. Any profession, and almost any specialty or subspecialty, includes persons of such diverse origins, education, experience, and interests that a newcomer always seems to be able to fit in without feeling too much a foreigner. Heterogeneity makes it easier for a newcomer to enter and also invites professional migration, for trying something new is such a frequent part of career development that movement often seems to be the norm.

Barriers to Mobility

Poverty keeps some young people out of college and thus keeps them from getting started on the road to professional levels of work and the personal advantages of upward mobility. The absence or the inadequacy of educational opportunities in some parts of the country has the same effect.

The high out-of-state tuition fees at almost all state colleges and universities are a deliberate effort to keep "foreign" students from benefiting from educational opportunities that are paid for by the citizens of a state. The students are more provincial or region-bound than they would be if all state universities dropped this policy.

Social custom has largely closed some careers to one or the other sex. Despite the law that bans discrimination on the basis of sex, women who enter engineering are about as rare as men who enter nursing.

Certification and credentials barriers inhibit geographic and occupational movement. Reciprocity exists among many states for some kinds of professionals, but state-by-state requirements—for example, in public

149

school teaching—often make it difficult to move across state lines. Guild restrictions make entry difficult if previous education or experience have not followed the guild's prescriptions.

At the Ph.D. level, narrow and highly specialized training may give a young scholar great power within his specialty, and at the same time limit the number and kind of jobs he considers appropriate. Attitudes developed in graduate school may also restrict the range of acceptable positions. Some young scientists looking for jobs have adopted the attitudes of some of their most prestigious elders in thinking that a full-time research appointment is the only truly respectable position for a scientist.

Finally, lack of information is a barrier to movement. In the United States we have a crazy quilt of channels of information about the availability of positions or of men and women seeking positions. We use published advertisements; commercial, university, and national placement services; private communications; and gossip. These means work, but surely with far less than perfect effectiveness. How many good connections are missed, no one knows. A man does not apply for a job he never heard of, and an employer does not offer a position to a man he never heard of.

Disadvantages of Mobility

Mobility also has some disadvantages. Frequent moves involve some fruitless motion, motion that Abelson has called "a feverish and wasteful game of musical chairs."[15] Men sometimes remain in a job too short a

[15] Philip H. Abelson, in testimony before the Senate Committee on Aeronautical and Space Sciences, 88th Congress, 1st session.

150

time to become fully effective. They may profit from their varied experience, but their employers sometimes do not get a fair return on the time and money spent in recruiting, inducting, and training the new but only temporary staff members.

Members of the family of a highly mobile man often pay a price for his mobility. The costs to his children are hard to count, but frequent moves may well interfere with their personal and educational development. Many a professional man has faced the choice of moving to a better position or of heeding the pleas of his high school daughter who wants to stay with her friends and classmates.

If the wife is professionally employed, she too must pay. Women with Ph.D.'s are likely to be married to men with Ph.D.'s. (In fact, the similarity of educational levels of husbands and wives in the United States is one of the strongest illustrations of assortative mating.) By great good fortune, a better offer elsewhere for the husband may coincide with a better offer for the wife, but this happy circumstance is rare. More often, when the husband accepts a new position in a different city, the professionally oriented wife must start afresh to hunt for a suitable position, or must retire from professional work. The slower rate of promotion, the lesser average salary, and the more modest professional accomplishments of married women with Ph.D.'s, in comparison with men with Ph.D.'s, are partly explained by the fact that their career decisions cannot always be determined by their own advancement and accomplishments but must be accommodated to the changes made by their husbands.

The Spread of New Ideas

A further automatic result, advantageous both to society and to individuals, of the movement of intelligent and educated workers to new regions, new employers, or new kinds of work is the rapid and widespread dissemination of new ideas and new techniques. University faculties are made more varied and lively by the presence of some members who have come from government or industry. Industry and government are similarly benefited by the presence of persons who have had experience in the other two sectors. When people migrate across disciplinary boundaries, they produce a healthy cross fertilization of ideas and techniques. A sociologist who is appointed to a law faculty brings new methods of approaching legal problems to his colleagues whose whole careers have been in the law, and they, in exchange, broaden his perspective. A physicist who engages in biological research brings to his new field a range of knowledge and a mastery of techniques that can add a new dimension to biological research.

In business, too, there are comparable advantages. It used to be rare for a business executive to return to a company he had left earlier. More and more frequently, however, large business concerns are finding it advantageous to reemploy former managers and executives who had gone to another company and acquired a different range of experience. One industrial consultant has explained that "as companies diversify, their need increases for men with the kind of broad business background that is sometimes not easy to get by staying at one company for a whole career. More companies seem to be realizing that a broad background, coupled with

152

familiarity with a company through previous employment, is a good combination for an executive to have."[16]

It is not easy to estimate, in any quantitative way, the extent of such stimulation and cross fertilization or how much this process contributes to the advancement of the nation's social and economic welfare. But Antonie Knoppers, a Dutch-trained industrial executive, has concluded that what is usually called the technology gap between the United States and Europe is partly a "mobility gap."[17] In Europe it is not as common as it is in the United States for scientists, engineers, or managers to move between laboratories and between different kinds of work, or for a man to work at different times in his life for government, for industry, and for a university. The result, Knoppers writes, is that in Europe there is more inbreeding and less ready exchange of information and ideas. Occupational mobility, in short, contributes to the continuing education of professional workers in a way that is advantageous to them and to the society that employs them. Patrick D. McTaggart-Cowan, executive director of the Science Council of Canada, in discussing American science policy gave credit to the high mobility of top men in research and development as a major factor in giving the United States an advantage over other countries in research and development activities.[18]

[16] Arch Patton (of McKinsey and Co.) quoted by Frederick C. Klein, "More Companies Relax Bars Against Hiring Their Former Employees," *Wall Street Journal*, Nov. 13, 1968, p. 1.

[17] Antonie T. Knoppers, "The 'Technostructure' Gap," *Interplay*, April 1968, p. 28.

[18] Patrick D. McTaggart-Cowan, Paper presented at 1968 meeting of American Association for the Advancement of Science, Dallas, Texas, Dec. 26-30, 1968.

Distribution of Quality

Still another advantage of mobility is that it serves as a quality selector, for able persons are more likely to move than are less able ones. The United States has long benefited from the selective aspect of migration. The people from other lands who migrated to the new country were certainly more adventuresome and probably more able than their fellows who chose to stay at home. Those who moved to the West were positively selected from among all who had settled in the older parts of the country. A century ago, Anthony Trollope commented on the American frontiersman: "I defy you not to feel that he is superior to the race from whence he has sprung in England or in Ireland."[19]

Migration is still a quality selector. In an analysis of migration patterns within the United States, Shyrock and Nam report that "within age, sex, and color groups, interregional migrants tend to be better educated than nonmigrants at their origin or destination."[20] In other words, people who leave one state, say New Jersey, to move to another state, say Ohio, are better educated than the average citizens of either state. Those who move in the other direction, from Ohio to New Jersey, are also better educated than the average in either state.

The United States is not alone in this respect. In Saskatchewan, Bennett found that "there is a tendency for the more ambitious and intellectually aggressive young men to leave in larger numbers than their more

[19] Anthony Trollope, ed. Robert Mason, *North America* (1st edn. 1862), Baltimore, Penguin Books, 1968, p. 87.
[20] Henry S. Shyrock, Jr., and Charles B. Nam, "Educational Selectivity of Interregional Migration," *Social Forces*, vol. 43, no. 3 (1965): 299-310.

cautious brothers."[21] Ritterband and Warkov found that scientists and engineers who migrate to the United States are on the average better educated than American scientists and engineers, and that British scientists and engineers who earned honors degrees were more likely to migrate to the United States than were their classmates who earned ordinary degrees.[22]

Folger, Astin, and Bayer analyzed the migration patterns up to 1964 of recipients of the Ph.D. degree in the physical, biological, and social sciences from American universities in the period from 1957 through 1960.[23] They divided these relatively young Ph.D.'s into five groups according to where they were when they finished high school, where they took the Ph.D., and where they went for their first post-Ph.D. job. "Where" in this analysis was one of seven geographic regions of the United States. The group as a whole did a good deal of moving. Over half made at least one interregional move between high school graduation and Ph.D., and 60 percent went to work in a different region from the one in which they earned the Ph.D. The authors called their five groups the "loyalists," the "recruits," the "defectors," the "returnees," and the "unattached."

[21] J. W. Bennett, quoted by Richard B. Woodbury, "Social Science and the Utilization of Arid Lands," Paper presented at the American Association for the Advancement of Science's International Conference on Arid Lands in a Changing World, Tucson, Arizona, June 3-13, 1969.

[22] Paul Ritterband and Seymour Warkov, "Foreign Trained Scientific and Engineering Workers in the U.S.: A Comparison with Their American Trained Counterparts," Paper presented at the Cornell Conference on Human Mobility, Ithaca, New York, Oct. 31–Nov. 2, 1968.

[23] John K. Folger, Helen S. Astin, and Alan E. Bayer, *Human Resources and Higher Education*, Staff Report of the Commission on Human Resources and Advanced Education, New York, Russell Sage Foundation, 1970.

155

The "loyalists" were those who graduated from high school, received the Ph.D. and accepted their first jobs all in the same region of the country. In terms of the quality of their graduate education—as judged by the ratings of the departments in which they took their doctoral degrees[24]—these students were, on the average, the weakest of any of the five groups.

The "recruits" made one move. They moved from the region of high school graduation to a different region for the Ph.D. and then stayed there for their first jobs. The "defectors" also made only one move; after graduating from high school and taking the Ph.D. in one region, they moved to a different region for their first jobs. These two groups were essentially the same in terms of the quality of their graduate education and both were somewhat better than the loyalists.

The "returnees" made two moves, one the reverse of the other. They left the region of high school graduation to earn the Ph.D. somewhere else, but then moved back to the original region for their first jobs. These returnees averaged above the defectors and the recruits in quality of graduate education.

The "unattached" also made two moves, but different ones. After graduating from high school in one region, they went to a second region for the Ph.D., and then to a third region for their first jobs. This group on the average got a better quality of graduate education than any of the other groups.

This analysis of ability has added a new dimension

[24] Allan M. Cartter, *An Assessment of Quality in Graduate Education*, Washington, D.C., American Council on Education, 1966.

to the consideration of interregional migration in the United States. Migration is usually discussed only in terms of the numbers of people involved and is most likely to be talked about in the regions that suffer quantitative losses. These regions are New England and the Midwest. The excellent universities of New England have long attracted superior students from other parts of the country, and the same is true of the North Central region, the home of such great institutions as the University of Chicago and the University of Michigan. Students flow into both for graduate study, and a few years later, with the credentials of a new Ph.D., go elsewhere for employment. New England usually accepts this situation philosophically and takes it as a tribute to the excellence of its universities—after all, Harvard, Yale, and MIT have been national universities for a long time—but in the North Central region there is considerable uneasiness about the "brain drain" from the Midwest to the two coasts.

Both regions do have quantitative losses, year after year, conferring Ph.D. degrees on more young scholars than they employ, but more is involved than the migration of a certain number of young scholars and scientists. When Folger, Astin, and Bayer analyzed the migration trends of young Ph.D.'s, they turned up the interesting fact that the several regions of the country show four different patterns of gains and losses. Some regions lose both quantitatively and qualitatively, that is, they educate more Ph.D.'s than they employ, and the ones they educate and then lose to other regions are on the average superior to the ones to whom they give first employment. This was the pattern they found in New England and also in the East North Central region (Ohio, Indiana, Illinois, Michigan, and Wisconsin).

The second pattern is one of quantitative loss and qualitative gain. This pattern was found in the West North Central region (Minnesota, Iowa, Missouri, the Dakotas, Nebraska, and Kansas). This region educates more young Ph.D.'s than it employs, but the Ph.D.'s from elsewhere who move in are superior to the Ph.D.'s who were trained there and then move away.

The third pattern is one of double gain, both quantitative and qualitative. It was found in the Middle Atlantic, the Southeast, and the Mountain and Southwest regions. All of these regions employ more and better Ph.D.'s than they educate.

The fourth possible pattern is one of quantitative gain but qualitative loss. This pattern appeared in the Pacific Coast region, which employs more Ph.D.'s than it educates, but which loses qualitatively on the exchange, for other regions of the country entice away a goodly number of the top-quality Ph.D.'s from such excellent universities as California, Stanford, and California Institute of Technology.

These quantitative and qualitative differences among the regions of the United States reflect both educational and labor market factors. Universities of the highest quality draw students from all parts of the nation. Universities of lesser note draw most of theirs from nearby. The more able students usually get the better scholarships and fellowships; they are more actively recruited by the better universities; and they are more likely to seek admission at the better universities. All of this means that the better students are more likely than the poorer ones to leave home to enter college or graduate school, and thus to take the first step that leads to the national circuit. The prestigious universities serve a national market; their graduates go far and wide. The universities of lower status—the ones which someone has called "institutions of purely local fame"—place most of their graduates nearby.

As a consequence of these differences, universities and students of the highest quality are elements of a national and even an international market, while universities of lesser note and students of lesser abilities are more closely bound to their own regions. The combination of educational selectivity and different labor markets explains the fact that regions tend to retain their poorer Ph.D.'s and export their better ones. The combination also tends to put the ablest persons, the adventuresome ones, the innovators, the ones with the best education, into national circulation where they can move into challenging positions and new areas of work and where they can stimulate and lead their colleagues to new achievements.

A consequence of these educational and labor market factors is that the best educated scientists—and probably other scholars as well—are more uniformly distributed over the country than they would be if there were less mobility. If graduate students always went to nearby universities, and if upon receiving their doctorates they then took nearby jobs, the regional differences in quality of scientific talent would be greater than they are now, with New England, the East North Central, and the Pacific regions even farther ahead of the rest of

159

the country than they are at present; and the Southeast, Southwest, and Mountain regions, farther behind. The parts of the country that cannot provide the highest quality of graduate education can employ a substantial fraction of the scientists who got that kind of education elsewhere.

International Migration of Talent

In recent years, significant numbers of physicians, engineers, and scientists have come to the United States from other countries. This immigration pattern differs substantially from earlier ones. The depression decade of the 1930's ended a century or more of massive immigration of unskilled workers. For the first decade of the twentieth century, immigrants averaged a million a year. From 1911 to 1930, the annual flow decreased to around half a million and during the 1930's plummeted to about 50,000. The number has since climbed back to about 400,000 a year, and as it has grown it has changed in character. Persons in professional, technical, and kindred occupations accounted for less than 1 percent of all immigrants in 1910, but for almost 10 percent in 1965. The real increase has been even greater, for in recent years more of the immigrants have been minors and dependents. Of immigrants who enter the United States labor force, persons with professional and technical qualifications have constituted from 10 to 20 percent in recent years.

In some professional fields, immigrants constitute a substantial addition to the American stock. Over a quarter of the medical internships in the United States and nearly a third of the residencies are filled by graduates of foreign medical schools. Many of these young doctors later return to their home countries, yet, as Kelly West has pointed out, we would have to build a dozen new medical schools to provide the equal of the 1,200 foreign physicians who enter the United States as immigrants each year. In most recent years the number of immigrant professionals in science and engineering, has exceeded 5 percent of the number educated in the United States.

The United States has not been alone in gaining the services of large numbers of professionally educated immigrants. In a period in which the United States received 372,000 professional and technical immigrants, Canada received 146,000, and Sweden, 90,000. The Swedish Committee on Research Economics has reported that 11.5 percent of all Swedish residents with university training were immigrants and that the percentages of persons with master's and doctor's degrees were, respectively, 13.5 and 19.0. Australia and West Germany have also been gaining well-educated immigrants. Among the reasons for the great increase in the professional component of migration flows to the United States and several other countries are the increased popularity of foreign study, easier and faster modes of travel, and higher levels of international communication, all of which have tended to internationalize the professional and scientific labor market.

Although the United States has not been alone in receiving large numbers of professionally trained immigrants, it has been the target of most of the brain drain criticism. Indeed a parody of a line from *My Fair Lady*—"The drain of brain goes mostly West by

161

THE USES OF TALENT

plane"—might well have served as the theme song for much of the discussion of the international migration of talent that took place during the 1960's. Britain's Minister of Health has insisted that "Britain simply cannot afford to train doctors for the purpose of swelling the membership of the American Medical Association." The Israeli Minister of Education has called emigrating scientists and engineers "traitors," and an American senator has called the whole United States experience with the immigration of professional manpower "a national disgrace."

Since these statements were made, two well-documented analyses have brought more rationality into the discussion. One was the report of an international conference on the large-scale migration of educated persons,[25] and the other was a report of an international study sponsored by Education and World Affairs.[26] Both of these reports have made the following points.

[25] Walter Adams, ed., *The Brain Drain*, New York, Macmillan, 1968. In August 1967 the Centre de Recherches Européennes of Lausanne and the U.S. Advisory Commission on International Educational and Cultural Affairs held, in Lausanne, Switzerland, an international conference on the "brain drain." The papers presented at that conference and an introduction by Paul Douglas are included in this excellent book.

[26] The Education and World Affairs studies were conducted or overseen by a committee consisting of Charles V. Kidd (The Association of American Universities), chairman; George B. Baldwin (International Bank for Reconstruction and Development); Frederick H. Harbison (Princeton University); John L. Thurston (Institute of International Education); Dael Wolfle (American Association for the Advancement of Science); and Robert L. Clark, the staff director. Reports of studies of individual countries and the committee's conclusions are included in *The International Migration of High-Level Manpower: Its Impact on the Development Process*, New York, Praeger Publishers, 1970. Two summary accounts have been published: George B. Baldwin, "Brain Drain or Overflow?" *Foreign Affairs*, vol. 48, no. 2 (1970): 358-72; and Education and World Affairs, *Modernization and the Migration of Talent*, New York, Education and World Affairs, 1970.

Individually, migration must usually be considered a gain. Men move across national boundaries for essentially the same reasons they move within a single country: to better their opportunities. The world as a whole has also gained. For centuries, migration has enabled men to take their skills and knowledge from places in which they were not being effectively used to places in which they could be better used. Receiving countries can still take this position, but losing countries often find it hard to adopt such a global view of the matter. They are losing physicians, engineers, scientists, managers, and other persons who were educated at the expense of the losing country and who are now going elsewhere to capitalize on that education instead of staying at home where they could contribute to the development of their homelands.

Being needed at home, however, does not guarantee effective use there. The critical question is not whether there is a need for improved health, better agriculture, further economic development, or better management, but whether the economy is able to employ people in such a fashion as to meet these needs. The major reasons for international migration are to be found in the countries men leave, not in those they enter. Britain, Norway, and Switzerland have lost significant proportions of their educated professionals, but France, Denmark, Finland, Sweden, West Germany, Spain, Italy, Yugoslavia, and Japan have not. Among the less developed countries, emigration has been high from South Korea, Taiwan, the Philippines, India, Pakistan, and Egypt, but many other countries have not had heavy losses. The difference lies in the ability of the home country to make use

163

of its educated manpower. As pointed out in Chapter Two, many countries have expanded their educational systems more rapidly than they have expanded their economies. They have provided higher education for more young men and women than they could absorb. Some countries in Africa and Asia which have not yet reached this stage are well on their way to it.

The implication of these analyses is that most of the responsibility for reducing the flow—if it should be reduced—rests with the countries that are losing their educated specialists. The opportunity to earn higher salaries is, of course, a reason for moving, internationally as well as nationally, but analyses of the causes of emigration place greater emphasis on the working conditions available to a professional man, on his opportunities to communicate with fellow professionals, on the opportunities to progress and advance in his specialty, and on similar nonsalary aspects of his professional life. Many professional men have been repatriated at substantial losses in income as soon as attractive professional opportunities became available at home.

This does not mean that there is nothing for the United States and other gaining countries to do. Health care in the United States should not continue indefinitely to depend so heavily on graduates of foreign medical schools. We could probably decrease emigration rates from some of the less developed countries if we supported first-class regional universities in the less developed regions instead of bringing so many students to the United States for training. In general, efforts of the wealthy countries to help the poorer ones will be either restrictive or ineffective if they are aimed directly

164

at preventing emigration. Excessive emigration is a symptom. Its causes are slow economic growth and the lack of favorable opportunities for professional employment and advancement. It is to these causes that the poorer countries themselves and the wealthier countries that are seeking to help them must give attention. Whenever migration rates seem too high, the primary scene of corrective action is in the countries of origin, not the countries of destination. George Baldwin, of the International Bank for Reconstruction and Development, concluded his analysis of the matter with the statement that "we can afford to be relatively relaxed about migration but not to be complacent about its causes."[27]

Conclusion

The policies and practices that make it easier for a person to leave one job and move to another whenever he decides that a move will be advantageous to him also make it easier for an employer who can offer more challenging opportunities, better working arrangements, or higher salaries to recruit professional and specialized personnel from employers who cannot match these attractions. Encouraging workers to move freely is advantageous to them individually, and helps to sort them into those positions in which their talents can be of most benefit to society. There are costs involved and not every move is advantageous both individually and socially. Yet on the whole, we have been able to utilize specialized and professional talent more effectively because people have been able to move freely to the jobs

[27] See note 26 above.

which they find most rewarding and in which their talents are most useful. It is good national policy to minimize the barriers and maximize the opportunities for occupational mobility.

6. Problems and Policies for the Future

THE United States has developed a flexible system for developing talent; the economy provides an extensive and varied array of professional positions; and reasonably effective means have been developed to adjust the available supply to the changing needs. But the whole system is rightly subject to some serious challenges. Perhaps the two most fundamental questions—questions that imply possibilities of radical social improvement—are these: How much good talent does the system miss? and Toward what ends do we want to direct it?

Lost Talent

Consider first the question of how much talent is lost. There is a sizable group of Americans who do not participate in or enjoy the benefits of the American system of educational and economic affluence. Joseph Kraft has put it this way:

> As an efficient machine, the American system functions as no other, and those of us who share in its products are lucky.
>
> But woe unto those who do not participate. If they cannot keep up with the national pace, they are cut off from education, decent housing, good jobs and even equitable treatment. They are out in the cold as in no other advanced country in the world.[1]

Mr. Kraft was speaking of all who are left out. Our focus here is on a smaller group of those who are left out:

[1] Joseph Kraft, syndicated newspaper column, Seattle *Times*, July 17, 1969, p. 11.

167

young people who have the potential, but who do not make it into professional careers. How many of them are there?

Much American folklore is based on the theme of rags to riches, or log cabin to White House. There is truth behind the folklore; many distinguished men and women have risen far above their humble beginnings; but at the same time many bright children have settled into dead-end jobs well below the levels they might have achieved. For some, the road has been from log cabin to city slum. There is good reason to worry about potentially high talent that remains undeveloped. Alfred Marshall said years ago that "there is no extravagance more prejudicial to the growth of national wealth than that wasteful negligence which allows genius that happens to be born of lowly parentage to expend itself in lowly work."[2]

How much lost talent is there? If we limit the answer to true genius, no one knows, but for a larger range of ability, an answer can be calculated. We know that college attendance rates are positively correlated with ability and with socioeconomic status. Figure 15 shows these relationships for the Wisconsin study, which was described in Chapter Four. Each line of the figure shows how college entrance rates were related to the ability of male high school graduates. The four lines show this relationship for four quarters of the total group, classified by socioeconomic status. The top line is for the top socioeconomic quarter. The three other lines, in order, represent male high school graduates whose families fell into the second, third, and bottom quarters in terms

[2] Alfred Marshall, *Principles of Economics*, 8th edn., London, Macmillan, 1930, book IV, chapter VI, section 5.

Figure 15
The Relation of the Ability and Socioeconomic Status
of 1957 High School Graduates in Wisconsin
to the Probability of Their Entering College

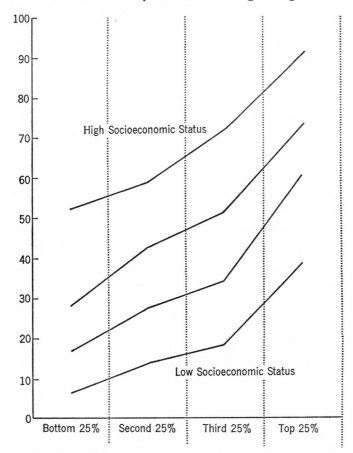

The four lines of the figure show, separately for each quarter of the group in terms of socioeconomic status, that at any socioeconomic level there is a positive relationship between intelligence and college entrance. Within any intelligence level (the four vertical sections of the figure) the probability of entering college is greater for students higher on the socioeconomic scale than for students from lower socioeconomic levels. SOURCE: William H. Sewell and Vimal P. Shah, "Socioeconomic Status, Intelligence, and the Attainment of Higher Education," *Sociology of Education*, vol. 40, no. 1 (1967): 1-23.

of socioeconomic status. Within each socioeconomic level, brighter boys were more likely to enter college than duller ones. At any ability level, boys whose parents ranked higher on the socioeconomic scale were more likely than their classmates from less favored homes to go on to college. Some of the differences are quite large. In the brightest quarter of academic ability, over 90 percent of the boys from top-level homes entered college. Boys of equal ability from the bottom socioeconomic level had only slightly better than a 50-50 chance of entering college.

We can start calculating the amount of lost talent if we assume that the top line represents the maximum reasonable expectations of college attendance. Young men at this socioeconomic level, or their parents, have the necessary money. They have known educated people and should know the advantages of education. Most of their parents have been reasonably well educated and are likely to have encouraged their sons to continue their own education. If they do not go to college, it is not for lack of opportunity. Realistically, therefore, we could not expect the percentages of college entrants from any of the lower socioeconomic groups to exceed the percentages from the top socioeconomic level.

Suppose now that we could erase all of the handicaps of lack of money, lack of motivation, lack of encouragement, and lack of academic interest that have held down the percentages of college entrants from the lower socioeconomic levels. If we could do that, we would move the three bottom lines up to the limit set by the top line. At each ability level, all boys, regardless of their home backgrounds, would then enter college with the frequency of boys from the top socioeconomic class.

As an example, in the Wisconsin case, from which the figure was drawn, the result would have been an increase of 52 percent in the number of male high school graduates who entered college. The same kind of calculations for girls result in an even greater increase, an increase of 80 percent in the number of Wisconsin girls who would have entered college in 1957. Continuing to use the same kind of calculations, we can see what would have happened if the effects of socioeconomic differences that are still influential after students enter college could have been wiped out. If after the Wisconsin students had entered college they had all remained and graduated with the same frequency as students of similar intelligence who came from the top quarter on the socioeconomic scale, there would have been a 58 percent increase in the number of male college graduates and an 89 percent increase in the number of female graduates.

The gap between what actually happens and these "iffy" figures is sometimes called "talent loss." Whether in an individual case the person would have been better off had he graduated from college is impossible to say. The "talent loss" group probably includes many persons who are at least as happy and who are working as effectively as if they had spent four years in college, just as the college graduate group includes some who would be as happy and effective had they not gone to college. Nevertheless, this analysis demonstrates that we could have more college graduates than we do if the "talent loss" group wanted to attend and had the opportunity.

171

The data and calculations just given were for one state, Wisconsin, and one year, 1957. College attendance rates have gone up since 1957, and the talent loss is now somewhat smaller. For the United States as a whole, including both men and women students, the Commission on Human Resources and Advanced Education estimated that in 1965 the number of college graduates would have been 50 percent greater "if all socioeconomic groups equaled the rates of the highest socioeconomic group in college attendance rates, in type of college attended, and in college completion rates."[3] In June of 1970, about three quarters of a million bachelor's degrees were conferred. Had all of the socioeconomic differences been wiped out, the number would have been over 1,100,000. It is not realistic to expect all socioeconomic differences to disappear; nevertheless, the 50 percent increase is an easy figure to remember as a kind of upper limit on the theoretically possible increase. Turned around, it means that the talent loss— as defined by not graduating from college—is about half as large as the talent trained through the baccalaureate level.

As an exercise in arithmetic, these calculations are reasonably sound, but as a basis for estimating the effects of social policy or as a basis for educational planning, they are pretty unrealistic. We are driven back to the question of why some students go to college and others do not. One easy explanation of why bright boys and girls do not go to college is that they lack the

[3] John K. Folger, Helen S. Astin, and Alan E. Bayer, *Human Resources and Higher Education*, Staff Report of the Commission on Human Resources and Advanced Education, New York, Russell Sage Foundation, 1970.

money. This is true enough for some, but it is not the answer for all. There have been no recent comprehensive comparisons of the relative importance of lack of money and lack of interest as reasons for not continuing on to college, but when Ralph Berdie conducted his study of this point in 1950, he found that among the top 10 percent of students the two reasons were about equally important.[4] If we assume that Berdie's findings are still applicable and that they apply to all high school graduates, we can assume that half of the students who might but do not go to college would go if they could afford it. We could get that half into college by a sufficiently large scholarship program, but the other half consists of high school graduates who do not want to go to college and would not go even if offered a scholarship. Thus it would be more realistic to say that if there were no financial barriers to college attendance, we might expect a 25 percent increase in the number of college graduates.

Even this figure is probably too high. Scholarships, loans, and work-study programs are much more generally available now than they were in 1950. We should assume that the increase in college attendance rates that has taken place since 1950 has included many students who could not have afforded college on their own but who got there by taking advantage of scholarship, loan, or work-study funds.

Thus, of the high school graduates who do not enter college now, it seems reasonable to conclude that more than half are not interested in college and would not be

[4] Ralph F. Berdie, *After High School, What?* Minneapolis, University of Minnesota Press, 1953.

173

attracted by a scholarship or loan. I do not know what
the exact figures would turn out to be, but I suspect
that we should be reasonably modest in our expectations
about the increases in college enrollment that could be
secured by increasing the amount of loan or scholarship
money available. Successful, but realistic, efforts to erase
socioeconomic differences in college attendance rates
would probably not increase the number of college graduates by more than 10 or perhaps 15 percent.

Within this group, whatever its size, there would be
some students of top quality. A few years ago, Norman
Crawford got in touch with a group of 1958-59 Merit
Scholarship Finalists whose parents could not afford to
send them to college.[5] His purpose was to find out how
many had gone to college and to determine the influence
of financial assistance on college attendance in this
select group. The students in question had a median
class rank among their fellow high school graduates at
the 96th percentile. Their mean scores on the Scholastic
Aptitude Test were 642 on the verbal portion and 661
on the mathematics portion. Clearly, these students
were good college prospects.

Two years after they had completed high school,
Crawford got information from 99.7 percent of the total
group of 1,550. He found that 1,336 had been offered
financial aid to go to college and all but 30 of these had
enrolled. He also found that 209 had not received any
scholarship or financial aid offers and that of these 209

[5] Norman C. Crawford, "Effects of Offers of Financial Assistance on
the College-Going Decisions of Talented Students with Limited
Financial Means," National Merit Scholarship Corporation, *Research
Reports*, vol. 3, no. 5 (1967).

students, 50 had not entered college. In percentage terms, 2 percent of those offered financial aid did not go to college, while 25 percent of those not given such offers did not get to college. Reversing the basis of comparison, we can say that the offer of financial assistance increased the percentage of students in this very able group who went to college from 75 percent to 98 percent. Clearly, this group is not representative of all high school graduates; they were far too close to the top end of the ability scale to be a representative sample. They are, however, an important part of the total and their record indicates that there are some very bright high school graduates who are still kept out of college by lack of money.

From the standpoint of policy, there are three conclusions to be drawn. First, the statistics are not a useful guide for planning for an individual. The decision whether or not to go to college should be an individual one. The student who happens to be born into a relatively poor home should have as much opportunity to attend college as does the student of comparable ability from a more favored home. From the standpoint of national policy, we want to eliminate socioeconomic barriers to college attendance even if we do not expect a large increase in the number of college graduates to result. Second, we can go ahead with efforts to remove, or to lessen, socioeconomic differences without worrying about flooding the market with college graduates. The increase would build up gradually, and the additional graduates could be absorbed into the economy. The third point is that if we want or need a larger supply of

175

college graduates, there is a larger potential supply available if we know how to take advantage of it. If we know how. Here is the catch. I have already pointed out that we really do not know how, for we do not understand well enough the influences that lead some students to college and steer other young people away.

The model of factors and influences that determine how a person's educational and occupational aspirations and achievements develop that was presented in Chapter Four made it clear that a large number of variables are involved and that they operate over a long span of years. But we do not know all of the variables involved, much less how to manipulate them. Except for those cases in which lack of money is the principal problem, by the time a student has finished high school it is usually too late to try to change his educational and career plans. His grade record is already compiled. His habits of study or of avoiding study are well established. His interests have developed, and it is not easy to change them suddenly. Parents and peers and other persons in the "significant others" category have already had their influences on his plans and hopes. In short, if we really want to eliminate the large talent loss, we must start intervening long before the time of high school graduation.

Contemporary social policy is a mixed one in this regard and will probably have to remain so for a considerable time. We are trying now to take remedial action at a variety of levels, from improved nutrition, Head Start and other programs for young children, up to special admission policies and special educational efforts at the college level. We can expect some success, but we must also expect some failures in these programs, for we do not yet know how to make any of them work as effectively as we would like.

In the long run, we can probably expect most success from efforts directed toward very young children. This is the thesis of Benjamin Bloom's *Stability and Change in Human Characteristics*.[6] Bloom points out that if we want to influence the course of development, the time to try is when development is going on most rapidly. If we want to stunt a boy's growth, we should not wait until he is six feet tall. If we want to stimulate a child's intellectual or academic interests, we should not wait until he is 18 years old. Head Start and other programs that are intended to help children overcome the handicaps of their own homes have been developed in recognition of the fact that interests, personality traits, and habits have their origins very early in life. If we wish to change a child's academic interests and motivation, that effort must also be started early in the child's life.

Merit and Diversity

Some students will strive to get to college, and some will be pushed there by their parents, but our policy is not to leave college entrance wholly to individual initiative or parental pressure. We have in fact developed two quite different sets of activities designed to bring into college some students who would not get there of their own accord. One of these sets of activities is based on a

[6] Benjamin S. Bloom, *Stability and Change in Human Characteristics*, New York, John Wiley and Sons, 1964.

policy of egalitarianism. Its two most notable expressions are found in the current efforts of many colleges to enroll high-risk black students and in the proliferation of junior and community colleges. The other set of activities is based on a policy of selection. It is exemplified by national, state-wide, and local testing programs and other efforts to identify high school students who show high potential but who because of their individual backgrounds or lack of parental encouragement would not otherwise be likely to enter college.

Both of these sets of practices have deep ideological roots. Both present some interesting psychological problems. Historically, the selection programs are the older. Psychologists can take credit for the development of the standardized tests of academic aptitude that have probably been more influential than anything else in calling attention to the range of human abilities and to the fact that persons of high ability are found throughout the entire range of wealth and social position. This is a professional accomplishment of great social importance. What the testers should feel guilty about is the narrowness of the basis of selection. Too many selection programs still rely too heavily on what amounts to the general factor of academic aptitude. The College Board *Review* has pointed out how much this concentration on general academic ability discriminates against music students. At the high school level, work in music is often not given academic credit. When the high school graduate seeks admission to college, he is usually required to meet the same standards in English and mathematics and academic aptitude scores as other students, and in

178

addition must meet whatever musical requirements are imposed by the Department of Music.[7]

By now there has accumulated a considerable amount of evidence on the diversity of talents possessed by students. The data from Project TALENT showed that while 16 percent of college freshmen scored above the 90th percentile level of high school seniors on a test of general academic aptitude, when three different tests were used to get separate scores on quantitative, scientific, and technical aptitudes, 35 percent scored above the 90th percentile on at least one of the three.[8] When Kenneth Little asked high school teachers to pick out their most talented students in mathematics, writing, and music, a considerable number of the students named were not in the top quarter of their classes in grade averages.[9] Because of a variety of evidence of this kind, I have elsewhere argued for the widest feasible diversity of selection standards and have contended that high ability in one area, such as music, or mathematics, or art, should always be allowed to compensate for lesser competence in other areas.[10]

The American College Testing Program has amassed a considerable amount of information about the musical, artistic, leadership, dramatic, and writing abilities of

[7] Arthur Motyeka, "Must Our Admissions System Punish Talented Music Students?" *College Board Review*, no. 69 (Fall 1968): 26-28.

[8] John L. Flanagan, et al., *The American High School Student*, Technical Report to the U.S. Office of Education, Pittsburgh, University of Pittsburgh Project TALENT Office, 1964.

[9] J. Kenneth Little, *A State-wide Inquiry into Decisions of Youth about Education Beyond High School*, Madison, University of Wisconsin, 1958.

[10] Dael Wolfle, "Diversity of Talent," *American Psychologist*, vol. 15, no. 8 (1960): 535-45.

179

high school seniors, as attested by the winning of awards or other marks of recognition. Traditional measures of academic aptitude were related to the kind of college a student entered, but these other kinds of ability were almost wholly unrelated.[11]

There is a great variety of work to be done in the world, and it takes a great variety of people to do all of it well. In simpler days there were various parallel channels toward success. Some men and women went to college; some served apprenticeships; others developed their competence through practice or independent study. There is an even greater variety of work to be done now, and more of it requires specialized forms of education or preparation, but not all of it requires a traditional college degree. We are, nevertheless, tending more and more to make college the only respectable gateway to a rewarding and prestigious career, despite the fact, as argued in Chapter Three, that the diploma is often used as a screening device and not as evidence of any essential change in its possessor.

Nostalgically, I wish that we could make apprenticeships and other forms of post-secondary education as respectable as going to college. Although realism argues that this is impossible, what we can do is to use wider and more diverse criteria for admission to college. There are more different kinds of talent than are measured by the College Boards.

The greater the variety of students we have, the greater is the variety of collegiate programs that we

[11] Leonard L. Baird and James M. Richards, Jr., "The Effects of Selecting College Students by Various Kinds of High School Achievement," *ACT Research Report* No. 23, Iowa City, American College Testing Program, 1968.

need, and this fact raises some interesting problems about the diversity among institutions of higher education. Many American colleges were founded to preserve the individuality of a particular group. Thus we have had Baptist colleges, Lutheran colleges, and Catholic colleges. We have had colleges for women, colleges for men, and coeducational colleges; colleges of divinity, colleges of music, technical institutes, and still other colleges for still other groups. Colleges that were founded to prevent the young of a particular group from being contaminated by contact with the secular world and those that were intended to preserve the individuality of the founding group were usually not very successful in achieving the intent of their founders,[12] and to a considerable extent many of these institutions have lost their individualistic character. In fact, it seems that nearly all institutions of higher education except the junior colleges—the great holdouts in this respect—are striving toward the same model, the complex, multipurpose university. Iowa State Teachers College has become the University of Northern Iowa, and Princeton has become coeducational.

One of the strong forces tending toward homogeneity is the grip the professions have on the undergraduate curriculum. The professional guilds of chemists, economists, physicians, psychologists, and other specialized groups exert a great deal of influence over their members in determining the kinds of research, the kinds of teaching, and the points of view that are approved by fellow members of the guild. As Jencks and Riesman

[12] Christopher Jencks and David Riesman, *The Academic Revolution*, New York, Doubleday, 1968.

181

have elaborated, the professions thus exercise a large amount of control over undergraduate education and tend to make that education pretty much the same in all institutions of higher education.

Nevertheless, there is still hope for diversity. Most colleges do not have the wealth to become instant Harvards. Public pressure will continue to insist upon unrestricted admissions to some institutions. Also students themselves select the institutions they attend, and there is still a considerable range of students. The American Council on Education, in analyzing large amounts of information on the freshmen who enter several hundred American colleges and universities, annually finds substantial campus-to-campus differences in student attitudes, aspirations, and abilities.[13] In terms of administrative policies, classroom practices, and other aspects of the institution and its faculty, there is also much variety among institutions of higher education, for faculty members and administrators of different colleges think of their roles and responsibilities in quite varied terms.[14]

With a substantial variety of institutions, a wide range of students, and the ability to collect and quickly

[13] John A. Creager, et al., "National Norms for Entering College Freshmen—Fall 1969," *ACE Research Reports*, vol. 4, no. 7, Washington, D.C., American Council on Education, 1969. Similar reports are published each year. Much material from this series of studies is analyzed in Alexander W. Astin, *The College Environment*, Washington, D.C., American Council on Education, 1968.

[14] Edward Gross and Paul V. Grambsch, *University Goals and Academic Power*, Washington, D.C., American Council on Education, 1968; and Patricia Nash and Sam D. Sieber, "The Goals of Higher Education—An Empirical Assessment," New York, Columbia University Bureau of Applied Social Research, 1968 (multilithed), compare the goals of different kinds of institutions of higher education as those goals are seen by faculty members and administrators.

digest large amounts of information about high school seniors who wish to go to college, a puzzle concerning policy arises. Is it better to encourage students to enter colleges in which they will be as similar to their classmates as possible? Or should we seek to maximize the variety of students on each campus? We are developing the means to provide admissions officers with much data concerning each applicant as well as the ability to provide each applicant with much information about prospective fellow students, grading standards, student customs, and other items of interest about a number of campuses. How should admissions officers and applicants use this information? Do we want one campus for hotshot young mathematicians, other campuses for playboys, still others for studious, industrious engineers, and yet others for the artistic and musical students? Or do we want to have as heterogeneous and varied a group as possible on each campus? There are arguments to support either course. What we have, of course, is neither extreme. Practically, however, what I am arguing is that we should strive to maintain a wide range of diversity of standards and educational environments.

Even at the top levels, maybe particularly at the top levels, we need to preserve diversity. A profession is always broader than any graduate department or professional school that prepares students for entry. New ideas may be initiated at the university and new knowledge is certainly generated there, but new tasks and new opportunities for applying professional competence develop in the field. Thus even in a department or professional school that is in the forefront in some respects, the education offered is typically narrower than the spread of activities found in the profession itself.

One reason why it is possible for a person trained in one discipline to move into another discipline is that each includes a wide range of kinds of work and responsibility. The more we narrow a field of work or scholarship in order to allow students to go into it deeply, and the more we make the field and the approach to it uniform from one school to another, the less effectively we are preparing students to move easily into new kinds of work and new responsibilities. In Chapter Five, I argued that a rather high degree of mobility is positively adaptive. I would add to the argument the claim that a reasonable number of the students who are preparing for work in each profession should receive a sufficiently broad education as to make it comparatively easy for them to switch from one subspecialty to another, from one kind of work to another, even from one field to another. This kind of education is not, however, the best kind for all members of a profession. The scholar who goes very deeply into his field, even into a narrow portion of that field, is the one who is most likely to add significantly to the basic knowledge of his field. The generalist seldom wins a Nobel Prize or makes fundamental additions to the knowledge of his field.

The specialist-generalist distinction is a further argument for a variety of educational programs. We need highly specialized specialists. We need generalists. We need people who understand the problems of a broad area or of several related areas. We need synthesizers. We need leaders. We need interpreters. They do not all come out of the same mold. We need a variety of molds in which to form them. Harold Benjamin argued this point twenty years ago in proclaiming that "that society which comes closest to developing every socially useful idiosyncrasy in every one of its members will make the greatest progress toward its goals."[15]

We need to encourage more intellectual anarchy in university departments. As one tactic directed toward this end, Jencks and Riesman have argued that whenever five faculty members, whether from one department or from several, decide that a new kind of specialty program is needed, they be allowed to start it.[16] The traditional departmental lines would not be destroyed by such an arrangement, and departments do serve a variety of useful purposes and should be maintained, but if five faculty members decide that it is time to offer a doctorate in the economics of natural resources management, or in the sociopsychological problems of newly developing countries, why should they not be given the opportunity? If the new program attracts no students, it will wither away. If it proves viable, a new need has been recognized and met.

This is not the only feasible approach. There may be better ways, for the Jencks and Riesman proposal skips over the problem of finding the added funds necessary to support new programs. Nevertheless, by one means or another, it is desirable to build into an institution that tends to be conservative and slow to change a recognized mechanism which will not only encourage change on a flexible and experimental basis, but which will also be hospitable to much diversity and to a variety of kinds of change.

In advocating college selection standards that would

[15] Harold Benjamin, *The Cultivation of Idiosyncrasy*, Cambridge, Harvard University Press, 1949.
[16] See note 12 above.

give greater weight to a diversity of special interests and abilities, and in advocating as great a variety of educational institutions and programs as we can achieve, I have actually been continuing to discuss the topic of lost talent. In a quantitative sense, we lose in the effective utilization of talent by failing to motivate and educate some potentially highly able young people. Qualitatively, we lose in the effective utilization of talent by defining too narrowly the kinds of talent we are willing to recognize, encourage, and educate.

The Selection of Goals

Charles L. Schultze, formerly director of the Bureau of the Budget, has projected the receipts of the federal government into the 1970's. On the basis of what seemed reasonable assumptions concerning the nation's Gross National Product, income tax levels, expected costs of military and defense activities, and other matters, Schultze expected federal receipts to go up more rapidly than federal expenses and thus to provide the nation with what he calls a "fiscal dividend." He has estimated that this federal surplus may amount to $38 billion in 1974, and *Fortune* magazine has extended the calculations to show a federal surplus of $90 billion in 1980.[17] These projections now seem overly optimistic in light of Federal receipts and expenditures for 1969 and 1970 and the budget for 1971. Nevertheless, we do have some options in the use of tax funds. If the economy

[17] Charles L. Schultze, "Budget Alternatives After Vietnam," in *Agenda for the Nation*, ed. Kermit Gordon, Washington, D.C., The Brookings Institution, 1968. See also *Fortune* magazine, March 1969, p. 91. Congressional decisions concerning tax rates and appropriations can quickly throw such projections out of date.

continues to grow approximately as expected, fiscal dividends should develop, even though they may not be as large or appear as soon as Schultze and *Fortune* anticipated.

One option would be to reduce taxes. Individually, we might welcome tax reductions greater than those in the Tax Reform Act of 1969, but collectively we may be better off if the fiscal dividend is used in other ways, for the nation has a lot of work to do that requires both large amounts of money and central government involvement.

The most detailed analysis of how extra federal income might be used has been carried out by Leonard Lecht of the National Planning Association.[18] Dr. Lecht started by collecting the statements of plans and goals for the nation that were formulated by President Eisenhower's Commission on National Goals, by special commissions and study groups appointed by later presidents, by acts and statements of Congress, and by such groups as the National Academy of Sciences. These were combined into sixteen goal areas concerned with health, education, housing, national defense, transportation, social welfare, consumer expenditures, space, international aid, and so forth.

As an illustration of the scope of these sixteen goal areas, the education goal assumes a 50 percent increase in the proportion of students from the eligible age group who receive high school and higher education; it allows for the doubling of faculty salaries in a decade;

[18] Leonard A. Lecht, *Goals, Priorities, and Dollars: The Next Decade*, New York, The Free Press, 1966; and Leonard A. Lecht, *Manpower Needs for National Goals in the 1970's*, New York, Frederick A. Praeger, 1969.

and it provides for increasing teacher-supporting staff, expansion of the adult education and vocational training roles of junior colleges, and increased plant and equipment at all levels of education. This goal is representative of all sixteen in that it is stated in terms of changes that can be quantified and that will cost money. These, of course, are not the only worthwhile goals. We want peace in the world and we want some of the inequities removed. Dr. Lecht recognizes these goals, but they were not the ones involved in his analyses.

If economic growth continues about as projected, during the decade that lies ahead we will have considerably more money than will be required to maintain health, housing, transportation, education, and the other goal areas at their present level, but there will not be enough money to achieve all sixteen goals at the levels that seem desirable.

Lecht then considered the numbers of workers who would be needed to achieve each of the sixteen goals. He calculated the number of teachers and professors, librarians and laboratory assistants, janitors and clerks, and all the others who would be needed to meet the education goal. Similarly, he calculated the number of electricians, airplane pilots, dentists, Navy officers, salesmen, secretaries, farmers, and all the other occupational categories that would be needed to achieve each of the fifteen other goals. His findings with respect to people were similar to his findings with respect to dollars. There will be more in 1975 or 1980 than there are now, but there will not be enough to achieve all sixteen goals. We will have to make some choices about how we want to utilize our human talents, just as we

188

will have to choose how we wish to utilize our economic wealth.

The conclusion that there will not be enough people should be contrasted with the projections presented in Chapter Two. Those projections were more conservative than Dr. Lecht's. He has taken a bolder approach. In essence what he has done is to ask: Suppose we set ourselves the task of improving the economy, education, health, transportation, housing, and other aspects of American life as much as we could in the decade ahead, how far could we go? How much money will be available to pay the large bills involved? And how many trained people will there be to do all of the work required? It is on this basis that he concluded that we would have neither enough money nor enough trained people to do all that we consider desirable.

However, he also concluded, and this is the hopeful part of the analysis, that we will have enough money and enough trained people to go a good way toward accomplishing what we consider desirable. If we have enough to do a lot, but not enough for everything, how should we deploy our resources? Clearly, such nationally important decisions must be made in the political arena of Congress and the executive agencies, and clearly there should be open public debate. This is neither the place to try to answer the question of how we should allocate our resources, nor the place to try to decide which goals to emphasize, but it is the place to indicate some of the implications of different decisions for the workers who will be required.

The different goals would make quite different demands on the American labor force. If we emphasize health goals, obviously we will need more doctors, dentists, nurses, hospital attendants, pharmacists, and others working in the health area. If we emphasize the transportation goal, we will need more airplane pilots, railway maintenance workers, and others. If we concentrate on the housing goals, we will need more electricians, bricklayers, architects, and other persons involved in the construction and building industries. If emphasis is given to improving the quality of man's environment, we will need specialists in ecology, land and resource management, economics, city design, energy generation, and pollution control, together with all the supporting personnel they require. A convenient method of illustrating the manpower implications of different goals is to consider the number of different kinds of workers who would be required if we were to spend an additional billion dollars a year on each of several goal areas.

Two such comparisons are given in Figures 16 and 17. Figure 16 contrasts the additional workers required by the health and education goals. Spending an additional billion dollars a year to improve health would require 24,000 additional workers in the professional health fields, mostly doctors, dentists, and nurses. The same amount of money spent on the education goal would require 39,000 additional professional workers, but professionals of quite a different kind, in this case school teachers, historians, physicists, psychologists, English teachers, and other faculty members. When we consider other segments of the labor force, other differences are found. The education goal would require more clerks, secretaries, bookkeepers, and other white

Figure 16
Numbers of Additional Workers Needed to Achieve
National Goals in Health and Education (in thousands)

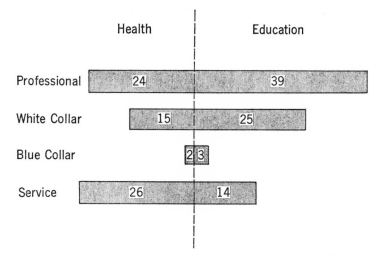

The additional workers needed if we were to spend an additional billion dollars a year to achieve national goals in health or education. Each bar to the left of the midline shows how many thousand additional workers of the indicated type (e.g., professional) would be needed if an additional billion dollars a year were spent on national health goals. The bars to the right of the midline have the same meaning for national goals in education. SOURCE: Lecht, *Manpower Needs for National Goals in the 1970's.*

collar workers than would the health goal. Neither goal would increase by very much the need for blue collar workers. In the service portion of the labor force, the health goal would require an additional 26,000 attendants, janitors, cooks, and waitresses, while the education goal would require only an additional 14,000 workers in this general category.

Figure 17 compares the health goal with the goal of urban development. Here the differences are more striking. The health goal would still require 24,000 addi-

191

tional professional workers; the urban development goal would require only about 3,000 additional architects and engineers. At the white collar level, the urban development goal would require 25,000 additional workers in comparison with the 15,000 additional ones needed to meet the health goal. The largest difference is in the blue collar category. The requirements of the health goal are small, but to meet the urban development goal, we would need an additional 43,000 carpenters, bricklayers, plumbers, electricians, and members of the other building trades and their counterparts in the factories that manufacture bathtubs, refrigerators, insulation, furniture, and all the other things that would be needed to build and equip the additional homes and apartments that would be constructed.

These two comparisons are sufficient to show that the priorities we assign to different goals will have a large influence on the numbers and kinds of specialized workers we need to attain our goals. It is altogether unlikely that we will select one goal area to the neglect of the others. We will push forward on all or several. Nevertheless, we cannot do everything that is desirable, and so some choices must be made. The basis for choice will be partly intuitive, partly political, and partly, perhaps, more or less accidental. High on the list of criteria will be the judgment of national leaders as to what is most desirable in the general interests of the country as a whole.

In reaching these decisions, one reasonable factor to be considered is the availability of the properly qualified kinds of specialists and workers, and the desirability of increasing the numbers of persons in one or another of the various manpower categories. For example, if we

Figure 17
Numbers of Additional Workers Needed to Achieve
National Goals in Health and Urban Development
(in thousands)

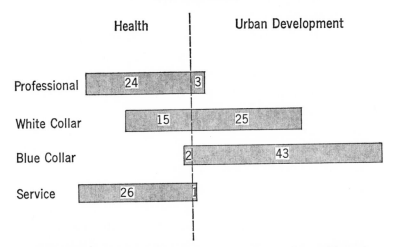

The additional workers needed if we were to spend an additional billion dollars a year to achieve national goals in health or urban development. Each bar to the left of the midline shows how many thousand additional workers of the indicated type (e.g., professional) would be needed if an additional billion dollars a year were spent on national health goals. The bars to the right of the midline have the same meaning for national goals in urban development. SOURCE: Lecht, *Manpower Needs for National Goals in the 1970's.*

decide that it is desirable to provide opportunities for a large number of persons to become competent members of the blue collar fields, emphasis on the goal of urban development would require so many more construction workers and members of the building trades that the long-standing practices of ethnic discrimination that have been followed by some of the craft unions would be forcibly broken down. There would be no other way to get the additional numbers of building craftsmen and industrial workers who would be needed.

In contrast, emphasis on the educational goal instead of the goal of urban development would create larger numbers of jobs in the professional, white collar, and service categories, and would have almost no effect on the blue collar category.

The relative priority we give to alternative national goals will have such substantial effects on national needs for different kinds of workers, specialists, and members of the different professions that we may wish to take these effects into consideration in establishing the priorities. Even if that is not done, the priorities will influence future demands. Some of the projections presented in Chapter Two and any similar projections will soon be obsolete if we decide to put a large amount of money into one or another of the sixteen national goal areas that Dr. Lecht has analyzed in detail. Within the last decade we have twice experienced exactly this situation.

The more recent experience resulted from the adoption of Medicare and Medicaid legislation. In this case, a massive national program suddenly called for expansion of the number of health workers. The domestic supply of physicians and dentists could not be increased quickly, but doctors came to the United States from other countries; American doctors worked longer hours and earned higher incomes; and the demand for nurses and hospital attendants increased.

The earlier experience was with the space program. Early in the 1960's, President Kennedy announced the decision to send American astronauts to the Moon and to return them safely to Earth before the end of the 1960's. That goal was stated without much prior con-

194

sideration of its implications for the American labor market. In retrospect we know that it moved a large number of men and women into new kinds of work. It increased greatly the frequency with which persons trained in one discipline crossed the border into another discipline. It attracted many scientists and engineers to the United States from other countries. It resulted in some new programs of university research and some new, but temporary, programs of graduate fellowships. Altogether, the decision to emphasize the nation's space goal brought about a number of widespread changes in the ways we have utilized our human resources.

We succeeded in achieving the space goal for a variety of reasons. We spent a very large amount of money. The space program had excellent leadership. And, most relevant to this discussion, the high mobility of a flexible, intelligent, educated labor force made it possible to get the job done. With a flexible labor force, including all of the relevant professional and specialized workers, we can achieve success in other high priority areas through essentially the same means we used in the space program. Whether in the process of setting national priorities we take account of their implications for higher education and the demands for high-level manpower, or go ahead without taking these factors into account, the effects on demands for various kinds of workers will be large and will differ greatly depending upon which goals we choose to emphasize.

The Need for a Sense of Direction

Any reasonable appraisal of the American system of educating and utilizing talent must come out on the

195

plus side. Faults there surely are—lost talent, discrimination, waste—but the system has also encouraged and rewarded ability regardless of its social origin. It has been flexible and powerful in adapting to the changing needs of society. On balance, the system, as a set of institutions, policies, and practices, must be given good marks.

If, however, one tries to appraise the ways we are using the system, there is much cause for worry. The schools of many cities are in decay, with strife sometimes at such a pitch as to make survival doubtful. The guerrilla tactics of a small minority of students and the justified dissatisfaction of a larger number interfere with work on many campuses. From conservative, socially oriented analysts to radical antiestablishmentarians charge after charge arises that our national priorities, the use of our industrial and economic might, and the use of much of our scientific and technological talent are directed toward the wrong goals.

The ills are evident. Their cures are not. The ills are, however, recognized, and there is a troubled groping for the sense of direction that will make it possible to develop cures. How we solve our problems of direction, goals, and social purpose is, from the standpoint of society, the preeminent factor that will determine how in the future we use our rich resources of human talent.

The Objectives of Manpower Policy

The future uses of talent will also depend upon another piece of unfinished business. Manpower policies and programs are constructed on pretty fragile foundations. We know too little to have much confidence that

196

new policies or changed practices will lead to the desired results. Sometimes there is even uncertainty about what we want to maximize.

Several criteria may be used to judge the soundness of manpower policies and practices.[19] One that has been used widely is the criterion of production. We have tried to determine whether or not there are enough engineers by asking whether or not industry would employ more engineers if they were available. Similarly, questions concerning the adequacy of the numbers of physicians, or school teachers, or other kinds of specialists have often been answered in terms of the numbers of filled or empty jobs, or in terms of production records, using the term *production* broadly.

A second criterion is that of self-fulfillment. An American dream has been to provide every child with the education that best helps him fulfill his own potential for development. That the dream is not always attained is painfully evident, but the degree to which we achieve it is one criterion of the effectiveness of our manpower policies.

A third criterion, which is of a different order from the first two, is cost. We devote a substantial fraction of our national resources to education. Some economic analyses have shown the money so spent to have paid good dividends both socially and individually, but some analysts have challenged this conclusion, at least in part, and some studies have shown some of our well-

[19] From this paragraph to the end of the chapter, I have copied and sometimes modified a portion of the introductory chapter to *Human Resources and Higher Education*. That chapter was written by the Commission on Human Resources and Advanced Education, of which I was chairman.

established beliefs about the comparative intellectual or economic virtues of different educational institutions to be largely myths. Perhaps even so we will want to increase educational expenditures, for economic return is not the only valid measure of value. Nevertheless, comparisons between costs and returns constitute a legitimate criterion for judging manpower policies and actions.

The final criterion, which is of a still different order, is the attainment of national goals. The goals of earlier generations were sometimes clearly formulated and supported by governmental action; an educated citizenry and the opening of the West are examples. But in recent years, with a central government of greatly increased power and with much of the labor force engaged in service instead of in production activities, there has been greater effort to plan and give explicit statement to national goals.

Many national goals have manpower implications. It takes more than a given number of men and women to achieve national goals; money and productive capacity and sometimes new knowledge are also required. But people are always involved, and the ways in which manpower decisions help or hinder the attainment of national goals constitute one criterion for judging those decisions. The objective of manpower policy is to help us get where we want to go. In this sense, manpower policy is analogous to economic policy. There are other similarities. Neither is a single policy but rather a complex of many policies dealing with various parts of an interrelated system of variables. Neither should have as its objective the establishment of rigid controls over all of the individual decisions involved, but rather the acquisition of enough knowledge of how a complex system operates to enable us to take the actions necessary to keep it in a healthy state.

We have not yet reached this level of understanding. There does not yet exist an adequate theoretical apparatus for predicting the results of actions in the manpower field, but there is beginning to be enough understanding of educational trends, market adjustment mechanisms, and the dynamics of human behavior to give hope that we can progress beyond pure empiricism. The development of a more adequate theoretical basis for policy will require the collaborative efforts of economists, psychologists, sociologists, and workers from still other disciplines.

Manpower matters are not determined in a completely decentralized fashion, and it is no longer safe to act as if they were. There is already enough concentration of influence in the federal government to make it urgent to try to understand the whole system better, for as influence becomes more concentrated and centralized, the penalty for mistakes increases. We should be pushing forward toward the development of a more detailed understanding and a theoretical formulation of the set of interrelated forces that determine the education and utilization of our major national asset, able and educated men and women. This task I commend to future students of the uses of talent.

Index

201

YORK COLLEGE OF PENNSYLVANIA 17403

0 2003 0084805 4